POPE
FRANCIS

Other Books by Chris Lowney

Heroic Leadership: Best Practices from a 450-Year-Old Company That Changed the World

Heroic Living: Discover Your Purpose and Change the World

A Vanished World: Muslims, Christians, and Jews in Medieval Spain

POPE
FRANCIS

WHY HE
LEADS
THE WAY HE
LEADS

Lessons from the First Jesuit Pope

CHRIS LOWNEY

LOYOLAPRESS.
A JESUIT MINISTRY
Chicago

LOYOLAPRESS.
A JESUIT MINISTRY

3441 N. Ashland Avenue
Chicago, Illinois 60657
(800) 621-1008
www.loyolapress.com

Cover illustration by Allan Burch

Hardcover

ISBN-13: 978-0-8294-4008-9
ISBN-10: 0-8294-4008-9

Paperback

ISBN-13: 978-0-8294-4091-1
ISBN-10: 0-8294-4091-7

Library of Congress Control Number: 2013948174

Printed in the United States of America.
15 16 17 18 MV 10 9 8 7 6 5

For the Angel who entered my life, bringing peace and joy.

Contents

1

The New Leader

Today's world stands in great need of witnesses, not so much of teachers but rather of witnesses. It's not so much about speaking, but rather speaking with our whole lives.[1]
—Pope Francis, Address from St. Peter's Square, May 18, 2013

There is no leadership training program for popes-to-be. Nor did some Vatican functionary hand Cardinal Jorge Mario Bergoglio the *New Pope Handbook* or *Pontificate for Dummies* as soon as white smoke started pumping into the Vatican sky to announce his pontificate as Pope Francis. Instead, as best we outsiders know, fellow cardinals applauded his election, vested him in white, gave him some prayerful privacy to recollect himself, then pushed (well, escorted) him onto the loggia of St. Peter's Basilica to assume leadership of 1.2 billion Catholics.

His actions immediately after were approvingly called "unprecedented and shocking" by the editor of *L'Osservatore Romano*, the semiofficial Vatican newspaper;[2] another Vatican reporter greeted a later papal initiative as "an epochal shift . . . a revolution."[3] Also, Pope Francis enjoys an approval rating that any other world leader would envy.[4]

Where did he learn to lead like this? Where does his vision come from? And what might the rest of us learn from him? That's what this book is about.

What Prepares Anyone to Lead Well?

After all, like the pope, we sometimes find ourselves thrust onto that metaphorical balcony: step up, it's time to lead this department, your family, this classroom, or, as the case may be, the whole Catholic Church.

Some folks approach such opportunities knowing that they are superbly prepared to lead, and that unshakable self-confidence stays with them every day of their careers. We call such people narcissists. They often get their organizations into trouble because, blinded by the radiant glow of their self-perceived greatness, they don't see what havoc they create or what misery they inflict on others.

Those of us with even a smidgen of self-awareness, on the other hand, quickly realize that no one fully trained us for the leadership challenges we inherit. Early in my own career at J. P. Morgan, I was trained to dissect corporate balance sheets and could ferret out companies that dared boost earnings by liquidating LIFO layers; I learned how to persuade corporate clients to save a few basis points by using our proprietary Eurobond structures instead of floating bonds in the United States.

I'm not sure I ever used either skill, and I've long forgotten how to do those technical stunts. After a few years at Morgan, I found myself as one of the managing directors in our Tokyo office, and in subsequent postings in Singapore, London, or New York, I never met a problem where liquidating LIFO layers was handy knowledge. And I quickly discovered that in the grown-up world, most problems don't have the same black-and-white answers as those pat bond-analysis equations.

Instead, I had to help the company figure out how to manage a large downsizing in the London office or how to motivate an unhappy subordinate. Now, some years after leaving Morgan and serving as board chair of one of America's largest health care and hospital systems, I have to offer modest advice and oversight as our superb management team navigates a rapidly changing health care landscape—shifting laws, new technology, ethical dilemmas, and a dozen other equally complicated challenges.

The skills I have most needed were not the narrow technical ones, but broader, all-encompassing ones, like making complicated decisions when the facts and my values collide; managing my priorities when fifteen things must be done before lunch; knowing when to play decisions safe and when to take major risks; and, ultimately, figuring out what is most important in life.

We Are Hurting for True Leadership

The complicated questions came more often, the time frames grew shorter, the ethical dilemmas more complex, and no one ever sent me to a leadership school that taught how to deal with any of that. Instead, my leadership school has been my life. Whether I learned my life's lessons well, my old Morgan colleagues and current health care colleagues would have to say. But I dearly hope that they would at least rate me better than average, because the average perception of leadership in America is truly awful. One major survey not long ago asked Americans whether they had a "great deal of confidence" in their leaders in politics, religion, business, or education. The answers? No, no, no, no. In not one of those four groups, considered bastions of our society, do Americans feel even *moderate* confidence.[5]

Granted, leaders nowadays have incredibly difficult jobs. They often are under-resourced, work under enormous time pressure, cope with frequent change, feel the glare of near-constant scrutiny and high expectations, and must motivate coworkers and stakeholders who often are skeptical of authority. These realities make it incredibly hard to lead.

But our disappointment—and frequently our downright disgust—with so many of our leaders stems from more profound factors than the role's sheer difficulty. Too often, those in leadership positions seem preoccupied only with their own status or income. They are unable to inspire or unite us; they are not imaginative enough to solve the seemingly intractable problems that plague us; they are afraid to make tough choices or even to level with us; and they are insufficiently courageous to lead us through challenge and drive change.

Bluntly put, something is broken. We need new ways of reimagining leadership and better ways of preparing ourselves and others to lead.

What Is Distinctive about a Jesuit Pope?

Enter Pope Francis, the Jesuit pope. The paradoxes begin right there. The Jesuits are a Catholic religious order of priests and brothers founded by Ignatius of Loyola and his companions in 1540. In the course of their improbable history, Jesuits cofounded one of the world's largest cities (São Paulo, Brazil), helped develop the Vietnamese alphabet, and helped institute the Gregorian calendar now used worldwide. They are the world's largest religious order that is fully integrated under one superior general; more than 17,000 Jesuits now labor in more than one hundred countries.

With that track record and global network, why is a Jesuit pope in any way paradoxical? Simply because the Jesuit founder detested overweening personal ambition. The Jesuit rule book, its *Constitutions*, decried excessive personal ambition as "the mother of all evils in any community or congregation."[6] And he instructed Jesuits to "promise to God our Lord never to seek" a high office in the Church, and, what's more, "to expose anyone whom they observe trying to obtain" a higher office.[7] Wow. Imagine if everyone in corporate America had to report ambitious colleagues. The sheer volume of reporting would allow no time to get any work done.

Ignatius wanted Jesuits to be humble because Jesus, their role model, was humble. But he also understood how ambition and political infighting can shred organizational morale (sound familiar, corporate colleagues?). So he was trying to rein in the human tendency to stroke one's ego by seeking status, power, and advancement.

Cardinal Bergoglio seems to have been a devoted son of his spiritual father Ignatius. After reportedly finishing as the runner-up in the 2005 conclave that elected Pope Benedict XVI, Cardinal Bergoglio didn't hang around Rome to build his network and credentials for the next election. Instead, he quickly headed back to Argentina, stayed out of the limelight, and devoted most of his time and energy to Argentina's poor (who don't get to vote for pope). He did such a good job of non-politicking that by the time of the next papal election, he barely registered on the list of conclave handicappers.

That's only one of the various paradoxes about the man's path to power and his understanding of power. If we need new ways to conceive leadership and how one prepares for it, the new pope gave ample food for thought in his first week alone. For example:

- His most intensive life and leadership training, other than his family upbringing, came from the Jesuits, a religious order that forms leaders not by management courses but in a month-long silent retreat, by sending trainees off on an arduous pilgrimage, and by preparing recruits to counsel adults by having them teach young children.

- Well known for his dedication to Catholic tradition, Pope Francis started dispensing with tradition within minutes of his election, refusing the traditional red cape (mozzetta), placing his own phone calls, and hopping onto a bus instead of into the papal limo.

- Within a few days of his elevation to the papacy, a position of enormous power and global prestige, he declared unambiguously that "authentic power is service."[8]

Will that unlikely background and those surprising first steps make him a great leader? No, certainly not by themselves. This book is no naïve cheer-leading exercise for him, his Jesuit background, or the Catholic Church. Pope Francis inherits a Church with wide-ranging, long-standing challenges: serious clergy shortages in dozens of countries, dwindling church attendance throughout the developed world, moral authority damaged by sex-abuse scandals, and, to judge by the public comments of various cardinals, a dysfunctional Vatican headquarters.

Such complex, multifaceted problems will not be resolved easily. Deep change will be needed, and the pope's early words and deeds make clear that he is committed to igniting massive culture change across his Church. Massive culture change? Isn't that a bit of hyperbole? Well, as exhibit A among many, consider what he told young Catholics gathered in Rio de Janeiro for World Youth Day: "I want you to make yourselves heard in your dioceses, I want the noise to go out, I want the Church to go out onto the streets, I want us to resist everything worldly, everything static, everything comfortable, everything to do with clericalism . . . May the bishops and priests forgive me if some of you create a bit of confusion afterwards."[9] Those are not the words of a man who is merely fine-tuning things. This pope is anxious to reinvigorate his institution and lead it energetically.

But even talented leaders find it difficult to drive change through organizations, all the more so an institution that appropriately cherishes its two millennia-old tradition. President Woodrow Wilson had it right: "If you want to make enemies, try to change something." Change agents certainly need competence and good judgment to succeed, but they also need courage, political savvy, iron will, and lots of luck.

So will he succeed? Only a fool would claim to know.

So why would the rest of us take leadership lessons from a pope with a yet-unproven record; from a Catholic cleric when we are Muslims, Buddhists, or even nonbelievers; from a religious leader when we are managing corporations, hospitals, or families; from a man who publicly kissed a young woman's bare feet when we would be locked up if we dared kiss a subordinate's feet at work; and from someone trained for years in Jesuit seminaries when we were formed in colleges, in business schools, and on the job?

Why We and Our Leaders Need to Change

Well, those are some of the very reasons we should take a closer look at Pope Francis's leadership vision, precisely because his leadership preparation and values are so different from what we have gotten used to. No, not just different but downright jarring, even "shocking" as that newspaper editor put it.

Let's face it: we badly need to be jarred from some of our settled preconceptions about leadership because they have utterly failed us. And we need to be shocked into new ways of thinking and acting. That so few of us feel great confidence in our political, educational, business, or religious leaders is an indictment, an extraordinary vote of no confidence across a broad swath of our society. Does anyone seriously believe that we will address such profound lack of confidence by the same old approaches in politics, business, or religious organizations? That's the old adage about insanity: doing the same things over and over, yet expecting different results. Nor will we close our leadership deficit by sending America's managerial class, elected officials, and pastors to one more leadership workshop, by tinkering with our performance-management systems, or through other incremental solutions. We need to be challenged to reimagine leadership in a turbulent, fast-changing, and sometimes unsettling new century.

The pope has already been articulating a vision that challenges his Church to reimagine itself in the twenty-first century:

- He challenged "lukewarm Christians" and "couch potato" Christians to engage much more energetically in spreading the Church's message, not to "take refuge . . . in a cozy life," but to get beyond our "comfort zones" and live with greater "apostolic fervor."[10]
- He challenged his Church to be more forthrightly "poor, and for the poor."[11]
- He warned Vatican diplomats-in-training that "careerism is leprosy."[12]
- He challenged a global culture in which "money . . . for the mighty of this earth, is more important than people."[13]
- He challenged his own fellow bishops to be "Men who love . . . poverty, simplicity and austerity of life."[14]

He asked Brazilian bishops bluntly, "Are we still a Church capable of warming hearts?"[15] Cardinal Timothy Dolan of New York, reacting to the pope's challenges, told an interviewer, "I find myself examining my own conscience . . . on style, on simplicity, on lots of things."[16]

Cardinal Dolan isn't the only one doing some soul-searching and reimagining. Pope Francis's words are resonating; his approval ratings have soared.[17] That fact alone is intriguing: he is fundamentally challenging our lifestyles and priorities, yet we are not dismissing him as a curmudgeonly old scold. Rather, we seem to appreciate that a plain speaker is telling us uncomfortable truths that we've long needed to hear.

But Pope Francis has done more than challenge his own Church; he is challenging our wider culture's whole approach to leadership by embodying a refreshing, deeply countercultural vision of how leaders live and what they value. He seems deeply self-aware and authentic, for example, while so many prominent public figures nowadays seem superficial and fake, constantly trying to spin us. The pope seems driven by a passion to serve, not by a craving for status, money, or power. Our culture is becoming increasingly self-absorbed and fascinated with superficial pursuits; he is striving to focus us beyond ourselves, on the struggles of our neediest brothers and sisters around the world. As I watched him, I started to wonder whether this unlikely choice for pope, even while igniting change in his Church, could be an equally unlikely catalyst for a long-overdue global conversation about leadership.

Perhaps he can inspire us to take on what might be called the new leader's habits. Cardinal Bergoglio literally donned a new habit, of papal white. And to lead well in this new century, the rest of us need new habits too, not literally, but figuratively—new ways of preparing ourselves to exercise leadership in our work and family lives. His call to lead his Church might invite profound reflection on the leadership call (yes, leadership is a call) that comes to each of us (yes, each of us), whether we live that call as chief executives, parents, or, who knows, as someday a pope.

And thus, this book about Pope Francis and how his Jesuit background has informed his leadership values and principles. It's not a biography. Plenty of those have already been written; yet, oddly, they have largely glossed over the Jesuit spirituality that prepared him to lead and still drives his thinking. Don't take my word for its critical importance; take his: "I feel like I'm still a Jesuit in terms of my spirituality, what I have in my heart. . . . Also, I think like a Jesuit."[18] Clearly, we can only understand this pope by first understanding what the following chapters explore: what it means to "think like a Jesuit."

But, in another respect, this book is as much about the rest of us as it is about the global leader of the Catholic Church. Pope Francis is our case study, a prism, the catalyst for us to ponder why we are so disappointed with the leadership status quo, to imagine an approach to leadership that would better inspire us, and to articulate the commitments we can make to become better leaders in our own lives.

Call to mind the vivid images that Pope Francis has already given us, and imagine them as scattered pieces of an important mosaic: a man bathes the feet of juvenile delinquents, kneels for fifteen minutes of solitary prayer on his first morning as pope, wears plain black shoes instead of red ones, wades into a crowd of refugees on the island of Lampedusa.

Our task is to assemble those discrete images into a coherent mosaic of new leadership. We have all been struck by what we have seen, but why? What are those images revealing about the nature of great leadership? Pope Francis's

Jesuit spirituality will serve throughout as our "code," a key to unlocking some of the underlying convictions that are driving him.

We'll work with three vital sources of information: first, what Pope Francis has been saying and doing; second, the leadership values he emphasized during his years in charge of Argentina's Jesuits or overseeing young Jesuit trainees (a number of them, now Jesuit priests, generously shared recollections and memories to allow us a privileged behind-the-scenes window into this man before the cameras followed him); and third, the principles that the young Bergoglio would have imbibed during his own decade-plus formation for the Jesuit priesthood.

It won't be hard to find convergence across these various strands of input. In fact, the common themes will virtually clobber us over the head. What emerges are six habits and convictions that surface again and again in Bergoglio's (and now Pope Francis's) life; his habits are implicitly a challenge to the rest of us: to commit to live similarly, and thereby to champion a new way of leading in our culture.

These commitments, taken together, are not a leadership formula or a bag of tricks but something far more basic, a fundamental leadership approach and worldview: how the leader sees himself and others, engages the world around him, and regards the past, present, and future. Jesuits and others might call this a "spirituality of leadership"—that is, the ways in which our journey through this earth becomes simultaneously a journey with and toward God (or our own understanding of transcendent meaning).

Subsequent chapters, always drawing on Pope Francis's life and formation, will explore these six foundational commitments of the new leader:

Know yourself deeply (chapter 3), but live to serve others (chapter 4):

- You cannot lead others unless you can lead yourself, so leaders dig deeply into themselves, confront their flaws, and, ultimately, achieve peaceful acceptance of themselves and the unique role they can play in the world.
- But, after that introspective deep dive within, leaders turn outward. They do not live for themselves alone but transcend themselves to serve

others. The wisdom and energy generated from their self-knowledge isn't bottled up but radiates outward.

Immerse yourself in the world (chapter 5), but withdraw from the world daily (chapter 6):

- The new leader immerses herself in the world with eyes open to its joys and sufferings and with hands calloused from sharing the everyday struggles of those around her. She is not apart and aloof but "in touch" and accountable. She cultivates solidarity, especially with those who are neglected or marginalized.
- Yet, while fully immersed in the world, she is not fully "of" the world. She does not drift on a tide of texts, media stimulation, and phone calls, but withdraws daily to reflect, feel gratitude for all she has, take in the big picture, and remind herself of her values and beliefs.

Live in the present and revere tradition (chapter 7), but create the future (chapter 8):

- The new leader seizes today's opportunity fully because it's the only opportunity he is certain of having. And he stands for something, honoring the beliefs and values bequeathed by his tradition.
- But deeply rooted in a tradition does not mean stuck. He is not enslaved by the past. He does not shrink from change fearfully but drives change with hope and optimism. He runs to the future, not from it.

A paradox seems to be emerging: each pair of habits verges on being contradictory. I must be immersed in the world yet withdraw from the world. I must stand for something yet embrace change. I must invest in knowing myself only to transcend myself and serve others. Well, there is something paradoxical and challenging about leading in this era of complexity and tumultuous societal change. Leaders need the good judgment to distinguish, for example, between an inviolable organizational value that can never be changed and a once-useful tradition that now must change. And leaders must willingly wade into the details of each day's complicated, painful dilemmas yet also step back to take a long-term, big-picture perspective. This dynamic tension is in fact what unleashes the commitment, imagination, and drive to surmount the complex problems we increasingly face in all walks of life.

That's why we need men and women who understand their calling in a very deep way and who have prepared themselves to lead by doing even more than acquiring technical virtuosity and superb competency in their chosen fields. Those are essential; without competent leaders we achieve nothing. But equally essential are the lifelong commitments just introduced, which make us leaders of depth, substance, and transcendent spirit. The very last thing we need right now are more easily digested tips or what the leadership industry inartfully calls "actionable takeaways." Our challenges are too big for that. And so, even as the following chapters explore Pope Francis's leadership convictions, these chapters simultaneously challenge us to ponder our own convictions and to commit to our leadership vocations in a more profound way.

Great Leadership Is Spiritual

Pope Francis's own attitudes about leadership are grounded in his Jesuit spirituality, and we will discover the broader relevance of that spirituality, whether or not one shares the pope's religious beliefs and whether one is a Jesuit or an investment banker. I say that with some confidence because I have been both a Jesuit and a banker. I underwent the same formation program as did Pope Francis, learned the same practices and principles he did, and if anything, those practices seemed more relevant and valuable to me in my post-Jesuit investment-banking years than during my half-dozen years in Jesuit seminary.

To be sure, for Pope Francis and the Jesuits, the values and practices introduced in this book have unambiguously religious roots. I have never met the pope, but I suspect he doesn't even have a "leadership philosophy"—instead, he focuses on one priority only: he is a follower of Jesus, and his Jesuit formation helps him follow Jesus more closely, end of story. This is what gives the Jesuit life meaning and purpose; Jesuits pursue their formation and spiritual practices for this end alone and no other.

Still, there are reasons the Jesuits and their spirituality (sometimes called Ignatian spirituality, after the Jesuit founder) have lasted for five centuries and been durable enough to serve Jesuits in virtually every cultural context and in countless occupations—whatever might "help souls," to use a shorthand version of their mission. The Jesuit founder envisioned a religious order plunged into the world, not sheltered in monasteries. Hence, he had to develop practices conducive to success amid the chaotic, distracting, tempting, confusing busyness that characterizes the work world. No wonder, then, that Ignatius's ideas are useful not only to Jesuits but to the rest of us as well, whatever our religious beliefs may be.

But if one need not be Christian or even religious to embrace this book's principles, one must be open to a paradox about great leadership: it is profoundly spiritual.

Yes, whether you are running a religious order or a manufacturing firm, are a devout Catholic or a secular humanist, great leadership is spiritual, and that vision will animate the ideas and practices promoted over the following pages—the very ideas and practices already demonstrated in the life of Pope Francis.

One of our J. P. Morgan chief executives used to say, "Our most important assets walk out the door every night." And so it is. The building you are working in, whatever its value on your organization's balance sheet, is surely valueless unless the people who enter and exit it each day know what they are doing, commit to the organization's success, are conscientious and dedicated, support their coworkers, make wise choices, honestly care about patients or students or customers, and exhibit a hundred other attitudes that make all the difference between success and failure. God knows, we can see those behaviors in action. But we can't touch or measure them; they don't find their way onto balance sheets. They are, in a word, spiritual.

Great leaders get this. They exhibit such behaviors themselves and inspire them in others. They are disgusted with the disgust our society increasingly feels about how leadership authority and power are wielded; the new leaders want to use their leadership power to steer our society and its organizations in a different and better way. That's what this book is about: the personal commitments that can guide and inspire the new leadership.

2

Of Spiritual Exercises and Cell Phones: Your Call to Lead

No. I did not want to be pope. Is that okay?
—Pope Francis, Address to Students, June 7, 2013

How does one prepare for leadership in the twenty-first century?

That question would elicit lots of different answers, but probably not this one: use a handbook from the sixteenth century.

Yet that's how Pope Francis prepared, and the beliefs and skills won through this sixteenth-century process turn out to be exquisitely relevant to twenty-first-century challenges.

A Very Specific Formation

I know a bit about Pope Francis's leadership formation because it was the same as mine. He was a Jesuit seminarian, and so was I. Though the pope's Jesuit formation was a continent away and a generation earlier than mine, the program and principles were nearly identical. Ignatius of Loyola mapped out that approach nearly five centuries ago, and its core has barely changed since. Some elements are what anyone would predict: during a Jesuit's first two years, the trainee, called a novice, studies Jesuit history and spirituality, settles into the order's culture and prayer routines, tends the sick, teaches catechism to children, and serves the disadvantaged.

But some of the training is uniquely Jesuit. For example, Ignatius prescribed that each novice spend "a month in making a pilgrimage without money, but begging from door to door at times . . . in order to grow accustomed to discomfort in food and lodging." Ignatius wanted to shake trainees free from their reliance on "money or other created things" and spur them to rely on God alone. The pilgrimage helped develop that attitude.[19]

But Ignatius saw other, more literal benefits to pilgrimage: he wanted tough, resilient Jesuits who could struggle through discomfort and overcome adversity. I'm reminded of my visit to Quantico, the Marine base where officer candidates are selected after a demanding regimen of physical and mental challenges. I asked the colonel what skills he was trying to inculcate. He mentioned a couple, paused to reflect, and then added, "You know, at the end of the day? The only thing I'm trying to do is to get these guys comfortable with the reality of being uncomfortable."

Amen to that. Modern life may have blessed us with every imaginable creature comfort, but, in a deeper sense, modernity can be pretty uncomfortable as we are buffeted by near-constant upheavals, wondering, for example, whether our job will still be there in ten years, or for that matter, in two months. Both Ignatius and that colonel seemed to have something similar in mind: equipping recruits with the attitudes that might steady them through adversity. American school children sometimes study seventeenth-century Jesuit Jacques Marquette, who founded Michigan's first European settlement and was the first European to explore hundreds of miles of the Mississippi River. His Jesuit formation came in handy: he had undertaken a two-hundred-mile pilgrimage as a novice in France, a warm-up act of sorts for his expeditionary adventure.

The pilgrimage had fallen out of favor by the time I began Jesuit life. Novice directors may have thought it an archaic relic of the medieval mind. But I'm happy that the tradition has since been revived. I recently read of American Jesuit trainees dropped off near the Haitian border with a prayer book, some clothes, and little else, and told to make their way to a town in the Dominican Republic. What better formation for sheltered young people, Jesuits or not, than walking a few days alone with their thoughts, unsure where their next meal or shelter is coming from, confronting the uncertainty and fears that well up, tasting what it feels like to be marginalized, and, ultimately, discovering their inner resilience. The pope repeatedly uses the metaphor of life as a journey: who can say whether his Jesuit formation may contribute to the prominence of that image in his mindset.

At the Center: The Spiritual Exercises

Whatever tinkering Jesuits may do around the edges of their formation process, however, one experience has never been shelved and certainly never will be because it is core not only to the novitiate, but to Jesuit life, and to Pope Francis's approach to leadership. The Spiritual Exercises is a series of meditations developed by Ignatius. Jesuit novices engage these exercises for an uninterrupted month, pondering Jesus' life, their personal history, and how they might follow Jesus in their own concrete circumstances. The month passes in near total silence, save for daily consultation with the novice director and an occasional break day. Jesuits work in more than one hundred countries, and every Jesuit of every generation has been grounded and molded by these Exercises. (I know of at least one young Jesuit in a country where Jesuits are forbidden from operating openly who did his Spiritual Exercises surreptitiously, meeting his novice director clandestinely in a home or a café for each day's spiritual guidance.)

These Exercises are almost certainly the most fundamental influence on the pope's spirituality. He has, after all, prayed and thought his way through their thirty intense days not once but multiple times: once during his own novitiate, then again some fourteen years later during the final phase of his Jesuit formation, and yet again as a novice director when he was responsible for guiding new Jesuit trainees through the Exercises. But that's not all: Jesuits must annually undertake an eight-day retreat based on the Exercises, a refresher, so to speak; Fr. Bergoglio not only made these annual retreats but also guided countless students, Jesuits, and others through variations of the program over the years.

Suffice it for now to introduce these Exercises and note their importance in the pope's life; their key themes will resurface in following chapters. Oddly—even inexplicably—the Exercises went almost completely unmentioned in the flurry of "insta-biographies" that emerged after the pope's election. Imagine, by way of analogy, a biography of President Dwight Eisenhower that never mentioned his military service or war experiences as contributing to his worldview and leadership style.

A Spirituality Designed for Frontiers

Jesuit formation differs from that of other religious orders in another important respect: it is long, *very* long. Jorge Bergoglio was ordained a priest more than eleven years after entering the novitiate; by that time, his contemporaries in diocesan seminaries had already been serving as priests for years. Not that Fr. Bergoglio was a slow learner; my own course to priesthood would have lasted a dozen years. A Jesuit joke: What gift does a Jesuit receive on his twenty-fifth anniversary in the order? They finally ordain him a priest.

The savvy Ignatius had reasons for the long formation. Consider the historical context. While most religious orders at the time were fully or partially monastic, requiring the entire community to gather for common prayer multiple times daily, Ignatius envisioned a much more activist model that was incompatible with daily common prayer. How well would a modern high school function, for example, if three or four times a day the full staff and faculty left to pray, abandoning a thousand hormone-charged teenagers to run amuck?

In fact, Ignatius broke down the monastery walls completely. Within his lifetime and after, Jesuits were regularly being dispatched to the world's frontiers: they were among the first Europeans to set foot in many Asian and Latin American locales, and they compiled Europe's first lexicons for a number of non-European languages. The expeditionary derring-do was peripheral, of course, to their main objective: engaging non-European cultures, typically through education, and presenting Catholic Christianity to people with very different belief systems.

That Jesuit frontier spirit enthralled a young Jorge Bergoglio, who joined the Jesuits with the hope of being assigned someday to work in Japan. That dream never came to pass, but the frontier vision still invigorates him. For his first formal visit to a Rome parish church, Pope Francis chose not a Baroque masterpiece near the Vatican but traveled to the city's very outskirts because, as he told the parishioners, "we understand reality not from the center, but from the outskirts."[20] A few weeks later, he told Jesuit journalists from *La Civiltà Cattolica* that "Your proper place is the frontier," the cultural frontier, where they were "not to build walls but bridges" to those who did not share Catholic beliefs or culture.[21] He told a group of devout Catholics that we should not "lock ourselves up in our parish, among our friends . . . with people who think as we do" but instead "The Church must step outside herself. To go where? To the outskirts of existence, whatever they may be."[22]

Pope Francis is striving to catalyze this same energetic frontier spirit in a Church he sees as too closed in upon itself; this is a key dimension of the overall culture change he envisions. He is, in some respects, implicitly hearkening back to his Jesuit forebears who did much the same in the sixteenth and seventeenth centuries. They pioneered geographic frontiers; Pope Francis is instead envisioning cultural frontiers in a postmodern era in which the Church has often been unable to communicate a message that resonates.

It's never easy to work on frontiers. We may be afraid of the risk or wander astray once out there. Consider the enormous challenges the early Jesuits faced. They often worked alone or in small teams. Guidance from headquarters was not a phone call away; in the very best case, a letter dispatched from Japan would reach Rome in many months, if ever, so Jesuits often had to rely on their own wits and judgment to resolve problems. The world as Europeans understood it had more or less tripled in scale in just a generation or two. And at home in Europe, as Martin Luther and other reformers successfully proposed new approaches to religion and spirituality, allegiance to the Catholic Church was melting away in one country after another.

The long, intense Jesuit formation program was Ignatius's ingenious solution to a host of head-scratching dilemmas that sprang from his commitment to immerse Jesuits fully into this world of disruptive change. Consider his organizational challenges: Can I so ground you in the values and culture that you will hold fast to them when you are on your own, halfway around the world? Can I get you so invested in our mission that you will always put the mission first—honoring management's judgment when you are dispatched to a distant mission yet fully capable of managing yourself independently, if necessary, once you get there? Can I endow you with a durable enough set of skills and attitudes that you will be capable of adapting on your own to each new situation?

As you reread the previous paragraph, squint just a little bit, and instead of seeing seventeenth-century Jesuits in Latin America, imagine any of us in today's fast-paced, complex environments. Aren't those exactly the same formation challenges that vex our attempts to mold change-ready, resilient employees—or for that matter, form our children to navigate their futures? Aren't these some of the challenges that the Church has to surmount in order to present itself effectively in today's world?

We've long understood that businesses, churches, schools, and families need strong leaders to guide them through tumultuous change. But, startlingly, we've spent relatively little time trying to understand just how to develop such leaders. Rather, we typically promote some smart, skilled person into a leadership role and then hope for the best. Well, hope is not a strategy. Ignatius of Loyola was instead willing to invest the time needed to equip his recruits with the commitments and habits that would turn them into principled, imaginative, change-ready leaders, and Pope Francis will be our case study as we explore some of those skills and habits.

The Ability to Make a Choice

One important skill, for sure, is the ability to make good choices, which was another advantage Ignatius found in the long Jesuit formation program: it forced both seminarians and Jesuits to make thoughtful vocation decisions. The seminarian had time to consider whether Jesuit life was truly his calling, and the Jesuits could watch each seminarian's performance in varying settings to assess his fitness for Jesuit life.

That long process proved a blessing both for me and for Jorge Bergoglio. It confirmed his priestly vocation and clarified my own choice to leave Jesuit life. After our respective novitiates and philosophy studies, we each taught in Jesuit high schools, the last formation step before theological studies and priesthood. He speaks of this as a happy, consoling time that confirmed his desire for priesthood.

Me? I enjoyed teaching and was fond of my students but gradually grew unhappy. I spent some time in denial of my feelings (I am, after all, a guy), then some time assuming that the unhappiness would eventually dissipate. But gradually I figured out it was time to heed Ignatius's decision-making wisdom. He explains that we certainly need to use our heads when confronting major life choices—we can't do something that we know to be illogical, immoral, or contrary to our beliefs. But we sometimes make bad choices if marooned in our heads alone, so we also have to use our hearts. That is, I had to confront my inner disquiet in some prayerful, reflective way and figure out what my inner feelings—or was it God's guidance?—might be indicating.

I could certainly rationalize the priesthood as a good vocation (my head at work), but was it a good vocation *for me* (my head and heart working together in a reflective way)? As often happens, as soon as I "decided to decide" by taking frank stock of what I was feeling and why, my decision came together pretty quickly. I know lots of priests who are very happy and peaceful in their celibacy, but that was a gift (or grace, or calling) that I did not have. I could have stayed and gutted it out with grim determination, but I would have been an unhappy priest, and the world doesn't need unhappy priests (or unhappy investment bankers, for that matter).

At the time I left, I was teaching economics in a Jesuit high school, and, brandishing that slimmest thread of a credential, somehow won a place in J. P. Morgan's management training program. During seventeen years there, I was lucky enough to serve as a managing director on three continents.

Not Just for "Spiritual" Leaders

During those first few months, my Jesuit formation seemed pretty irrelevant and even occasioned an embarrassing moment or two. For example, though Jesuits take vows of poverty and technically own nothing, they can be oddly possessive of their dinner napkins: after dinner, each Jesuit carries his cloth napkin from the dining room and tucks it into a cubbyhole labeled with his room number, then reuses it for the following meal. My seven-year napkin habit proved hard to shake. Early in my J. P. Morgan life, I sometimes became aware of a colleague shooting me a curiously sideways glance as we strolled out of the corporate dining room, I in my pinstripe suit, absentmindedly clutching my paper napkin as if bearing it to my very own cubbyhole.

It was more than these idiosyncratic incidentals that didn't quite fit my new world. Ignatius of Loyola had counseled us to "love poverty like a mother" because it was the "strong wall of the religious life."[23] Then I got my first bonus check, and, at least for a while, prosperity seemed a more loving mother than poverty ever had been. Still, Ignatius had a point: he noted how the possessions we own can end up owning us, and I watched with amused wonder over the years as various colleagues ratcheted up their lifestyles with each new bonus check—the new house, then the second house, then the second, fancier car—until prosperity ultimately enslaved them; they had to keep earning investment-banker wages; they had no way off their lifestyle treadmill.

But I was so caught up in these obvious differences between Jesuit and "worldly" life, such as napkin cubbyholes and a vow of poverty, that I long overlooked eminently transferable skills and attitudes that were entirely relevant to my new life: knowing how to make good decisions, adapting to new environments, dedicating oneself to goals bigger than self, knowing oneself, and a dozen other attributes that we know are essential in contemporary organizational life.

The trouble is, we don't really know how to teach these in the corporate arena because they are not cookie-cutter skills. And even though Ignatius had figured out how to transmit such skills, I didn't really perceive their value until tumultuous, rapid change made their value unmistakably apparent.

My path to enlightenment began the afternoon that the future walked into our J. P. Morgan offices in the form of two or three senior executives from Ericsson, a Swedish telecommunications company and a long-standing J. P. Morgan client. The company had been founded in the 1870s by a Swedish gentleman (Mr. Ericsson, naturally) who repaired telegraph equipment. Ericsson had grown and prospered for decades, thanks to the utterly reliable and utterly sleepy business of manufacturing equipment for telephone systems.

Except this afternoon, Ericsson's executives seemed to have lost their minds. They wanted to move aggressively into a new business line and wondered if we would invest alongside them. The concept? Cellular telephony. Instead of landline telecommunications signals running through wires, airborne radio waves would be relayed along transmitters atop towers. Telecommunications would become completely mobile. Humans, untethered from phone cords, would place calls from cars, restaurants, parks, or anywhere else within signal range.

We weren't idiots at J. P. Morgan (have I mentioned that *Fortune* magazine regularly rated us America's most admired bank?); we knew about mobile telephony. But for the first time, at least in my department, it was a concrete business proposal, not improbably futuristic technology. After the Ericsson executives left, we huddled to pick apart their proposal. We were skeptical. Those prototype cell phones looked ridiculous, as large as bricks—who was going to lug one of those around in a briefcase? Why would anyone even need one? I had a phone in my office and a phone in my home; would I ever really need to make a call while commuting from one place to another? Above all, massive investment (that's where we came in) was required to jump-start the system: the continental United States spans some three million square miles. Who was going to finance cell phone towers over all that real estate, betting on a technology with no proven market?

So we passed on the deal. At first, our skepticism seemed well founded. The only people who lugged around those unwieldy phones were prima donnas thrilled to hear themselves say, "I'm calling you from the back of the limo; we'll be at your office in about ten minutes."

But within only a few years, it became laughably obvious that we wizards at America's most admired bank had gotten it badly wrong that day. As it happens, meetings like ours were happening all over Morgan and all over the world during that year and every year since. Waves of new technologies are cascading over us: in mobile Internet, robotics, telemedicine, genetics, the automation of knowledge work, 3-D printing, and energy production, to name but a few. They are changing everything from how we do our jobs to how we monitor our health to how we pay for our morning coffee.

The changes are so rapid and wide-ranging that not even the savviest executives know for sure what their business will look like in five years. Jeff Bezos, who knows a thing or two about emerging technologies as Amazon's visionary founder, likens our era to the dawn of the electric age: a powerful new force is at our disposal, yet we are at only the earliest stages of knowing how to use it.[24] That thought is invigorating: if this is the beginning, imagine what might come. But that same thought is also terrifying. Where is all this headed? What is the implication for my life? And what about my children's lives?

We're learning something counterintuitive about what it will take to thrive amid superfast, supercharged technological change, namely, *it's not primarily about the technology*. That is, no one can possibly master the details of every rapidly emerging technology, year after year. So the first skills we need to master are more fundamentally human ones, like how to make difficult decisions amid uncertainty, how to stay focused amid swirling daily chaos, and how to keep track of ultimate goals when day-to-day demands continually distract our attention. A recent *Chronicle of Higher Education* report, for example, noted that the job skills most lacking among candidates for professional positions were by no means technical, but, "adaptability and managing multiple priorities, and making decisions and problem solving."[25]

Early in my managerial career, whenever we met to evaluate our rising junior executives, one would hear phrases like "She's great at the numbers" or "His analytical skills are superb." Those skills alone might distinguish standout performers from weak ones.

Those narrow technical skills remain essential but are now almost taken for granted, an entry ticket of sorts. As the business environment became more complex, and the pace of change quickened, one started to hear very different phrases at our managerial-evaluation committees: "She can't deal with ambiguity. She needs too much direction." Or, "He doesn't like change, is afraid to take initiative." Or, "He's a lone ranger. He won't play on the team or support other departments."

In fact, we started assessing individuals against criteria that once would have been reserved for chief executives alone, such as, "This person has no sense of vision about where this organization should be going." Or, encapsulating all the above: "This guy has to show more leadership if he wants to thrive here."

What Makes a Leader, Really?

That's why this book is not just about Pope Francis but about all of us. Like it or not, "show more leadership" is the ineluctable fallout of what we are living through and will be confronting for the foreseeable future. Early in my Jesuit life or my J. P. Morgan career, whenever the word "leadership" came up, we thought of a person: the Jesuit General or Morgan's chief executive. They were the "leaders" of these respective organizations. And the scale, complexity, and pace of change were manageable enough that a small handful of individuals could in fact lead their groups or companies effectively.

But as technological and social change unfurled, our concept of leadership necessarily changed too. "Leadership" no longer brings to mind the one person in charge but a set of behaviors needed from every person. After all, the dictionary tells us that leaders "show the way . . . by going before or along with." They "guide or direct, as by persuasion or influence, to a course of action or thought." Note that "being in charge of lots of people" does not feature in this basic definition. I often tell attendees at leadership conferences to imagine four words stamped onto their foreheads: *direction, influence, choices,* and *results.* They are not effective leaders by virtue of climbing the organizational ladder but by modeling those four words in whatever platform life presents them, starting with the platform they have right now, be that parent, pope, or junior hire straight from college: everyone has the chance to lead by manifesting a sense of direction, exerting positive influence on others, and accepting accountability for results.

Let's think about our seventy-six-year-old Argentine pope, for example. By some conventional measures, let's be frank, he doesn't seem so well prepared for what he has inherited. He has never worked in the "headquarters" he now oversees; he was accountable for 2.5 million Catholics in Buenos Aires, and now for 1.2 billion worldwide. We are living in a wired world, and in one book-length interview, he self-deprecatingly described himself as not very competent with the Internet and joked that he might pursue it more in earnest when he retired.[26]

But he has nonetheless been leading us energetically and effectively. Long before he preached his first sermon, he had started "showing the way," as that dictionary definition of leadership puts it, with gestures like hopping the bus instead of the limo, forsaking a golden pectoral cross for his plain metal one, and stopping his pope-mobile to embrace an obviously disabled man. We all got the message about what the Church should be about: be humble, be simple, take care of the poor, neglected, and marginalized. In ensuing days, he gave words for those deeds; phrases like, "How I would like a poor church, and for the poor" and "authentic power is service" started rocketing around the blogosphere.

And his willingness to make choices that broke from tradition has already been influential, another element of great leadership. One Vatican cardinal, Peter Turkson of Ghana, said that the pope's simple lifestyle and focus on the poor "would mean that we [in the Vatican Curia] need to reconsider our lifestyle."[27] The pope had not issued a single directive to his team about lifestyle and may never have to. His actions may have spoken for him. That's leadership.

In a technologically driven century, the pope's technology skills are pretty deficient. But in a leadership-starved new century, the pope's approach seems incredibly well suited to the broader demands of leadership. If we commit to approach life and work similarly, we will lead effectively too. Now we delve into six commitments of the new leader.

3

"A gift to live fully": Be Who You Are

Do not be afraid! We are frail and we know it, but he is stronger!
—Pope Francis, Address from St. Peter's Square, May 18, 2013

A veteran Vatican reporter, taking stock of the early months of Francis's Papacy, wrote, "In terms of public opinion, Francis is already on the cusp of achieving the iconic status of Nelson Mandela, a figure of unquestioned moral authority."[28]

Only time will tell whether that comparison will prove apt, but this much is certainly true of both men: we admire them, in no small part, because of their integrity, the way in which they have led their own lives. Their leadership inspires others because of their *self*-leadership, and their respective paths to self-leadership involved deep introspective journeys. That inward journey is not always easy, witness the confession attributed to Nelson Mandela: "My greatest enemy was not those who put or kept me in prison. It was myself. I was afraid to be who I am."

That quote jarred me. South Africa's first black president, father of his reborn country, always seemed anything but afraid. He languished for nearly two decades in Robben Island's desolate prison blocks, his bed a mat on the floor, entitled to one visitor a year and to receive one letter every six months. He pursued the only work his jailors allowed: swinging a hammer to break big rocks into smaller rocks, day after day, year after year.

Countless rocks were crushed, but his spirit wasn't. His example calls to mind another great human rights activist, Dr. Martin Luther King Jr. who observed of his own tribulations: "As my sufferings mounted, I soon realized that there were two ways that I could respond to my situation: either to react with bitterness or seek to transform the suffering into a creative force."[29]

So it was for Mandela, who emerged from prison not embittered but gracious and embarked on his life's most important mission at age seventy-two. He articulated a vision for a renewed South Africa, inspired or cajoled sometimes skeptical compatriots to embrace it, sowed hope and enthusiasm, and did it all with such charisma, courage, and self-confidence that he quickly became a living case study: see, this is how a person leads.

It's hard to imagine this man saying, "I was afraid to be who I am."

I used to think that only a few of us were intimidated by the challenge of stepping up to lead, but I've since learned that we are legion. I've often displayed Mandela's quote in presentations to business leaders. While they read the quote, I read their faces and see how closely Mandela's confession hits home, so I'm never surprised when one or two of them confide as much while unwinding later over a beer. Yes, these men and women, many of them highly successful in very demanding professions, are a bit afraid too.

Blissfully Unaware?

Only those who have never been troubled by an introspective moment manage to bluster ahead blissfully, fearless because they are clueless about their own weaknesses and the consequent risk of shipwrecking their families or companies by dumb choices. The conscientious, in contrast, sometimes agonize about the potential implications of mishandling the challenges that life thrusts on us, such as how heavy-handedly to intervene in an adolescent child's troubles, whether or not to fire the underperforming subordinate instead of giving a third (or fourth) chance, how to motivate a demoralized teaching staff, or how to resolve a looming budget gap.

The introspective impulse can seem like a burden—wouldn't I lead more confidently if I didn't dwell on my insufficiencies for the task or the collateral consequences of my actions? But that introspective impulse, pursued further, ultimately liberates and empowers the leader, a "deep dive" that brings the blessing of self-acceptance, or, as Mandela might put it, the courage to be oneself. Yes, I'm flawed but more so gifted. All in all, I'm a unique person with a unique role—the spiritually minded might even say a calling—to lead in some capacity. I'm flawed, gifted, and called to lead: these convictions, in dynamic tension, are what invigorate the healthy leader, and this chapter is about the inner work that yields such convictions.

I thought of Mandela's words—"I was afraid to be who I am"—while reflecting on Pope Francis's first moments as pontiff. Granted, the pope hadn't apprenticed on a prison rock pile; he was cardinal of a large, infinitely charming, and (at times) equally chaotic metropolis. But, like Mandela, he faced significant challenges, assuming leadership of a Church that even friendly supporters labeled "in crisis," or, at best, "badly in need of reform."

There were reasons to be intimidated by the task ahead: he had never worked in the Vatican and was surrounded by prelates who had not only made careers there but took great pride in safeguarding its intricate protocols. I wonder how heavily the burdens of history and tradition weighed on this aging man as they ushered him into the appropriately nicknamed "Room of Tears" to recollect himself before he was introduced as the Catholic Church's new pope. No institution reveres tradition so deeply as the Church. In many workplaces, you hear things like "This is the way we've always done it before"; Catholics get used to hearing weightier expressions, like "the unchanging tradition handed down from the apostles." Tradition is never trifled with lightly.

Be Your Best Self

All the more stunning, then, that Pope Francis dispatched with tradition nearly a half-dozen times in his papacy's first two hours: eschewing the red papal cape (the mozzetta); keeping his own simple pectoral cross instead of choosing from the more precious ones offered him; greeting the faithful in St. Peter's Square with an informal "good evening" instead of more formal language; asking the crowd's prayer for blessing before bestowing his own; and, at the end of it all, leaving the papal limo empty to join his fellow cardinals on the bus.

L'Osservatore Romano, the staid newspaper of record for Vatican watchers, called the performance "unprecedented and shocking."[30]

Except it wasn't a performance at all. We were not watching someone trying to act like a pope. We were watching a person unafraid to be who he was: Jorge Mario Bergoglio, called to serve as pope, not someone donning a costume to play a new role. In fact, if anything discomfited him at all, it seemed to be only the costuming, apparently a bit too regal to hang comfortably on his shoulders.

Over those first forty-eight hours, two acquaintances made the same exact observation to me: "Wow. That guy seems really comfortable in his own skin." Yes, that's it exactly. Be comfortable in your own skin. Know who you are, the good and the bad. And find the courage not just to be yourself, but the best version of yourself. These are the foundations of self-leadership, and all leadership starts with self-leadership because you can't lead the rest of us if you can't lead yourself. And you can't lead yourself if you haven't done the work to know who you are.

Not everything you find will be pretty. Everyone is flawed; the demons of self-centeredness, hunger for power, fear, or lack of confidence stalk every leader. Leadership, therefore, is not merely knowing yourself but manifesting the will to battle your demons. After all, if you have not struggled to tame your own weaknesses and become the best version of yourself, how will you credibly challenge the rest of us to be better versions of ourselves?

But no one overcomes every weakness, and the introspective deep dive is not finished until you find peaceful self-acceptance, the conviction that you have a unique and worthy contribution to make despite your flaws. Only when you believe this about yourself will you convincingly motivate the rest of us to believe it about ourselves.

The Power of Loving Acceptance

In the course of writing this book, I communicated with a number of Jesuits who had lived or worked with Fr. Bergoglio. I wanted to see the leader "off stage." How a leader projects in public is one thing, but how he treats his colleagues when the cameras stop rolling is a much more revealing insight into his character. I was particularly interested in those who had been trained as young Jesuits under Fr. Bergoglio's tutelage; his vision about leadership would emerge most clearly in the priorities and values he tried to inculcate in these trainees. Fr. Hernán Paredes, an Ecuadorean Jesuit now working in New York, was one of those I interviewed, and among many anecdotes and insights he shared was this one: "For him [Bergoglio], it was important that we love and accept ourselves the way we are." It was Fr. Bergoglio's more profound articulation of the conviction just introduced: leaders must find peaceful self-acceptance, the conviction that they have a worthy contribution to make, their flaws notwithstanding.

Think of these two quotes, then, as the bookends of this transformative inner journey that precedes any serious effort to lead. "I was afraid to be who I am" marks those who have not yet come to grips with themselves in the ways just outlined. "Wow. That guy is really comfortable in his own skin" marks those who have done the work and are ready to lead.

In between? The tough but rewarding inner work that yields a bundle of related qualities that have become ever more prominent in the leadership literature over the past couple of decades: self-awareness, integrity, authenticity, and character. Self-awareness is the foundation of the others: I can be authentic, true to myself, only if I know myself, what I stand for, and what I ultimately think humans are here for. And integrity is nothing more (or less) than understanding that I cannot honor such truths selectively; I must lead a "whole" life (the root meaning of the word *integrity* is "whole") not a split life. That is, I can't ask subordinates to behave one way yet behave differently myself, be a loving parent at home and a tyrant at work, give you my word today and not honor it tomorrow, profess certain values in church or mosque yet not embody them at work. What does personal integrity look like? Alejandro Gauffin, a Jesuit priest who studied under Fr. Bergoglio a quarter century ago, watched the pope's first few days and told me this: "Everything I see from the new pope now, everything I hear now . . . I saw then, and I heard then . . . It is like reliving our days together in the parish, when he taught me that gestures were worth much more than words."

Those who master this bundle of personal qualities—integrity, courage, authenticity, respect of self and others—lead with character. And the many who don't even bother trying or who consider character a soft, ill-defined notion that matters little as long as the leader is technically competent? Well, we can no longer afford leaders who don't appreciate the importance of character. It is time to consign them to the dustbin of history; they get us into too much trouble.

Don't take my word for it. Take it from those who have led men and women in some of the toughest situations on earth. General Martin Dempsey, chairman of the Joint Chiefs of Staff of the United States military, is accountable for a $500 billion annual budget and for leading more than two million people. Military leadership carries the highest possible stakes: if executed poorly, human beings may die. Here's General Dempsey's bottom line: "You can have someone of incredible character who can't lead their way out of a forward operating base because they don't have the competence . . . and that doesn't do me any good. Conversely, you can have someone who is intensely competent, who is steeped in the skills of the profession, but doesn't live a life of character. And that doesn't do me any good."[31]

The late General Norman Schwarzkopf, who led coalition forces during the first Gulf War, said something similar: "Leadership is a potent combination of strategy and character. But if you must be without one, be without strategy."[32]

Their blunt pronouncements won't surprise anyone who has worked in contemporary organizations, where we are suffering an epidemic of the opposite, whether it's the reptilian types who never quite become comfortable in their skin because they are too often shedding it, or the chameleons who camouflage naked ambition by saying one thing today and a different thing tomorrow as they slither through the corporate jungle. What's most authentic about them is the one thing that they don't want to display plainly: the rest of us matter only if we can help them get ahead.

So even though they may "talk the talk" of teamwork, mutual respect, and putting mission ahead of self-interest, it never quite convinces. We hear the words but never quite see the deeds, and few things are as corrosive as that mismatch. Readers are likely picturing their favorite corporate villains while reading these few sentences, but this plague afflicts organizations of all sorts. Look, for example, at how bracingly the new pope has confronted his own Church: "Inconsistency on the part of the pastors and the faithful between what they say and what they do, between word and manner of life, is undermining the Church's credibility."[33]

Leaders who don't know themselves, or aren't true to themselves, can't lead effectively because they have forfeited what should be a leader's most powerful tool: integrity, the power of personal example. Without it, the leader is implicitly saying, "Do as I say, not as I do," which is hardly inspiring. Stripped of the power of example, they must compensate by relying on fear, manipulation, authority bluntly wielded, or paying us to follow because they cannot inspire us to follow. With integrity, on the other hand, the leader's life becomes a simple, elegant statement: "Follow me." When I asked Fr. Paredes what he learned from Fr. Bergoglio, Paredes paused for a minute, shrugged, and simply said, "Probably I learned from him, just by looking at him . . . I wanted to follow that man, to be like him, I wanted to do things the way he did them, whether saying Mass or chores or anything else." That's what leadership with character looks like.

The fallout from characterless leaders is severe. Witness as one example the survey conducted annually by the prestigious global public relations firm Edelman, which asks respondents across two dozen countries whether they trust leaders to "tell the truth, regardless of how complex or unpopular it is." The findings? Only 18 percent of respondents around the world trust business leaders to tell the truth, and only 13 percent trust government leaders to tell the truth.[34]

A civilization erected on such fundamental mistrust cannot possibly thrive in the long run. That's why we're appropriately swamped with a wave of management books beating the drum for greater leadership integrity. Trouble is, it's far easier to champion integrity than inculcate it. Teaching competence is far more straightforward than engendering character. We understand well how to teach even intricate skills, like conducting neurosurgery or engineering hundred-story skyscrapers, but we are less certain how to teach someone to lead a health care system or a construction firm with character. Helen Keller the first deaf-blind American to earn a bachelor's degree, argued that "Character cannot be developed in ease and quiet. Only through experience of trial and suffering can the soul be strengthened, ambition inspired, and success achieved."[35]

Self-Knowledge Forged by Personal Challenge

I know any number of leaders whose sense of themselves and their life direction was forged in the crucible of personal challenge, including, apparently, Pope Francis. After resolving to enter the seminary, he explained that he had a wilderness experience, a "passive solitude"[36] endured without any apparent reason or precipitating crisis. What exactly was going on inside him? He doesn't elaborate. Perhaps he simply felt stranded: still in the world but uninterested in pursuing worldly delights or a career and not yet able to start pursuing his destiny in seminary. Not long after, he ended up facing a very literal crisis. He fell seriously ill at age twenty-one, at one point nearly dying of a lung infection. With an abnormally high fever, serious pneumonia, and three cysts eating away at his right lung, he hovered near death and asked his mother in a frightened panic, "Tell me what is happening to me . . ."[37]

Here's how he reflected on that experience years later. "Suffering itself is not a virtue, but the way in which it's taken on can be virtuous."[38] As a Christian, he understands Jesus' cross as the "seed of the resurrection," and in some analogous way then, his whole understanding of suffering is based on a similar sense of "transcendence. . . . It is a gift to understand and to experience suffering fully. Even more, it is a gift to live fully."[39]

The pope's understanding of suffering is, of course, deeply informed by his Christian beliefs. But humans have been grappling with the mystery of suffering since long before Jesus walked the earth. As the Greek tragedian Aeschylus put it, "Wisdom comes alone through suffering." Pope John Paul II compared suffering to "a bitter kernel containing the seed of new life."[40] By no means do we intend to exalt suffering or make a fetish of it: would that we lived in a world where no child ever suffered. But the mystery nonetheless remains that challenge, setbacks, failure, and even suffering come to all of us, and these trials introduce leaders to themselves. They force us to discover not only our own resilience but to reflect on our deepest sense of self: why am I here and what do I want from life?

And if life doesn't thrust a moment of self-scrutiny upon us, we need to find some other way to make the deep dive that will yield the core convictions about self that every leader needs. But how to get there?

Well, we can start with a straightforward question: what do you believe about yourself and your place in the world?

A Simple Personal Creed

That's what the pope did. Shortly before his ordination as priest, the thirty-two-year-old Bergoglio wrote out a short credo (the word means "I believe") in a moment of what he called "great spiritual intensity."[41] He has kept the paper ever since, showing it to an interviewer nearly four decades later. It's neither a theologically precise creed like the ones Christians recite in church, nor is it a sterile philosophical treatise that one might defend as a dissertation.

Instead, he wrote it as if planting a stake in the ground that would always remind him of his core convictions. It is deeply personal, and, therefore, wonderfully idiosyncratic; it reflects his Christian beliefs, but always through the prism of his own concrete history. Not, for example, "I believe in an afterlife," but, as he wrote it, "I believe that Papa [his father] is in heaven with the Lord."[42]

What a powerful exercise: record in about 200 words, less than a page, your deepest beliefs and aspirations about yourself, your key relationships, humanity, God, and your role in the world. What a great investment in self-awareness! And how interesting it would be to pull out that paper from a folder every few years to ponder what has or has not changed.

Fr. Bergoglio's creed may have been written in an impulsive moment of inspiration before his impending ordination, but the habit of self-reflection had by then been deeply ingrained by his Jesuit formation. He had been through the month-long Spiritual Exercises and through weeklong annual retreats, and pursued a regimen of reflection to keep him on track daily.

And, while his creed may at first glance seem a near-random string of ideas, upon closer look, dominant themes become apparent, a set of interrelated convictions about himself that are also core to the Spiritual Exercises, and, once adapted to accommodate each person's religious beliefs, core convictions for any leader.

First, *I am flawed.* The thirty-two-year-old Bergoglio is painfully aware that he is weak and fallible, or, as Christians would put it, a sinner. His creed confesses the "egotism in which I take refuge" and the "pettiness of my soul that seeks to take in without giving . . . without giving."[43]

Second, *I am a good and gifted person.* No hint of self-loathing or despair flows from his frank self-assessment of his flaws. Strikingly, quite the opposite. He seems optimistic and happy: "I look forward to the surprise of every day . . ." he writes.[44] He accepts himself completely, perhaps because he feels fundamentally affirmed and loved: "I believe in God's patience, welcoming, good like a summer night . . . I believe in Mary, my mother, who loves me and will never forget me."[45]

What's more, he knows he has gifts to offer the world, starting with the most basic gift that every human being is capable of offering: "I believe in wanting to love much . . . I believe that others are good and that I ought to love them without fear, never betraying them in order to seek my own security."[46]

Third, *I am called to offer my gifts,* to play a unique role, to lead. Bergoglio's creed references a decisive incident from the year he turned seventeen, so compelling that he still recalls the date: September 21. On his way to a picnic with friends, including a woman to whom he was quite attracted, he stopped in a church, happened to make a confession to a priest he had never met before, and was so deeply moved that he resolved that morning to change his life path completely. He would abandon plans to become a pharmacy technician or a doctor and instead, a few years later, enter a seminary. He walked out of the church and headed home, leaving his friends waiting at the train station.[47] His creed recalls that moment: "I believe in my own life history, which was pierced by God's look of love, and . . . leading me to an encounter in order to invite me to follow him."[48]

Flawed, gifted and fundamentally good, and called: the three convictions are dynamically related. It's not merely, "Hey, I'm flawed. I'm arrogant and impossible to work with. But I've accepted myself, and I'm going to live authentically as my arrogant self. So you ought to accept me too." No. The call to leadership embeds not only acceptance of self but acceptance of the accountability to become the best possible version of oneself by addressing one's flaws relentlessly; the call to lead inspires that ongoing commitment to self-improvement.

Nor, on the other hand, is it, "There is a calling and role for me, but only if I can first manage to transform myself into an impossibly perfect, superhuman version of myself." No. The summons to lead begins now, with the person I am now.

Anyone familiar with Jesuit spirituality would immediately perceive how Bergoglio came by this worldview because the opening week of the Spiritual Exercises reinforces exactly the same dynamic.

Flawed Humans, Flawed Lives

First, we humans are flawed. Well, that's how you or I might put it. Ignatius, reflecting the religious imagination of his era, put it a lot more bluntly: "I will look upon myself as a sore and abscess from which have issued such great sins and iniquities and such foul poison."[49] Clear enough? In case his Jesuit trainees don't get the point, Ignatius has them meditate on their sinfulness not just once but various times.

Many readers won't relate to language about personal sinfulness; some will wonder why they are reading about sin in a book that explores leadership. But whatever a person's beliefs, we can agree on this much: humans are weak, flawed, and prone to the sway of inner demons such as greed, self-centeredness, and petty resentments. No one can lead well without knowing and confronting his or her inner demons. Without confronting and coming to grips with these ugly aspects of ourselves, we are kidding ourselves or those around us, inauthentic people who lack the depth of character needed to lead.

But someone who feels worthless will not lead well either. These early meditations on sin don't climax in morose self-pity, but, as Ignatius puts it, in "an exclamation of wonder and surging emotion."[50] Not only am I still here—my "sins and iniquities" notwithstanding—but I'm destined to an exalted role, to co-labor as God's partner in the business of turning the world into what it should be, a place where every human person gets the chance to flourish in dignity.

These same core convictions resurface continually in Jorge Bergoglio's life. Only a few years after writing that credo, he was named head of Argentina's Jesuits, their "provincial" in Jesuit-speak, at the extraordinarily young age of thirty-seven. As provincial, he was one of fewer than 300 Jesuits privileged to convene in Rome in 1975 for the order's 32nd General Congregation, the Jesuits' highest governing and strategy-setting forum, momentous because convoked on average less than once a decade. One of the decrees approved by Bergoglio and the other delegates, called "Jesuits Today," sought to describe "Jesuit identity for our time." Here is its opening sentence: "What is it to be a Jesuit? It is to know that one is a sinner, yet called to be a companion of Jesus as Ignatius was . . ."[51] The idea should by now be familiar: flawed yet called.

Take a moment to marvel, by the way, that a whole organization's core identity would open with a humble confession of frailty. I long worked in an institution that prided itself on being America's most admired bank; we proudly parroted J. P. Morgan Jr.'s claim that we only did "first class business, and that in a first class way."

Some colleagues basked a bit too much in the reflected glow of our firm's reputation, imagining that the chest-thumping was about them personally. Our irreverent assessment of these arrogant souls? "This guy is starting to believe his own b———t." Other colleagues, conversely, managed to rise even to the heady stratosphere of senior management yet not lose a balanced perspective on themselves. That sense of self improved their leadership; secure in their strengths and fundamental worth, they freely acknowledged their weak spots and asked colleagues to complement these. That sense of self inspired loyalty, sometimes earning one of the highest plaudits that jaded investment bankers are willing to offer their managers: "Hey, she didn't forget where she came from."

Well, the very same could be said of Pope Francis. His consecration as bishop in 1992 marked his own ascent into the Church hierarchy's stratosphere. He chose the motto that he now bears as pope: *Miserando atque eligendo*, that is, "Having mercy, he called him." The phrase references the Gospel story in which Jesus calls Matthew, a tax collector, one of a detested breed who enriched themselves by squeezing pennies from near-penniless peasants. Matthew was therefore a shocking choice as an apostle, a flawed man pursuing a morally reprehensible occupation. Yet Jesus, "having mercy," calls him to contribute his talents in some special way (Matthew 9:9).

That motto crystallizes Pope Francis's core self-understanding: a flawed man who has nonetheless been invited to offer his unique gifts to an important task.

As the saying goes, "You can't give what you ain't got." Bergoglio had to understand himself, his unique dignity, and his calling before he could lead effectively in the world.

A Teacher Who Understood Flawed but Accepted

And, watching his style of interacting with students and Jesuit seminarians over the years, we might say, "Because true leaders understand themselves, they can form others." Take the case of Roberto Poggio, a young high school student who in the 1960s attended the Jesuits' prestigious Colegio del Salvador, where Fr. Bergoglio was teaching literature and psychology. In a personal interview, Poggio recalled one incident during his senior year. "It happened during some sports match. I slapped a younger kid, the kind of thing that happens in sports, nothing out of the ordinary, and a typical 'youth brawl' happened." Fr. Bergoglio found out about it, and "he asked me to show up the next day in one of the classrooms at a certain time."

"So when I get there, I see ten of my best friends sitting in a circle, and Fr. Bergoglio sitting off to the side. He told me I should tell my friends in detail what had happened, and it became something that stuck with me for life. They were understanding, they gave advice, and somehow I felt as if a load had been lifted off me—I felt no reproach or attacks from them." Fr. Bergoglio never intervened but merely watched as Poggio's friends ran the meeting and eventually decided the appropriate punishment: Poggio was suspended from sports for two weeks and had to call the younger kid out of class to apologize for what he had done.

I, too, taught in a Jesuit high school as part of my training, and I "busted" plenty of teenagers for misbehaving. I typically meted out some absurd punishment or other, forcing them to sit idly in a classroom for an hour, for example. At best I engendered their regret for misbehaving, at worst their embarrassment in front of friends and resentment toward the school. How foolish I feel, in retrospect, looking at what human development Fr. Bergoglio managed to squeeze from one childhood fistfight on the playground. I focused only on reforming errant behavior; he focused on forming a young person to lead life well. Every theme of this chapter was encapsulated in microcosm as he brought together Poggio and his classmates, then trusted them to orchestrate their own mini-seminar on human frailty, on dignity, on assuming leadership, and on accepting the call to be a better version of oneself. That's not my conclusion; it's Poggio's. Here's how he summed up the episode: "Jorge Mario Bergoglio was above all a person who helped to draw the best out of each one of us, who really raised our self-esteem."

Nor was that the priest's only creative attempt to do so. When Hernán Paredes told me that Fr. Bergoglio wanted the Jesuit trainees under his supervision to love and accept themselves as they are, I pressed for some detail, an example of how he transformed those nice-sounding words into deeds.

Paredes shared a curious example. He had been among a handful of young Ecuadorean Jesuits who were sent to study at the Colegio Máximo San José, a large Jesuit-run seminary complex on the outskirts of Buenos Aires, then managed by Fr. Bergoglio. Though Paredes didn't put it this way, it sounds as if the Ecuadoreans, plopped down among scores of Argentines, were sometimes regarded as the newly arrived hicks in cosmopolitan Buenos Aires. One of Paredes's Ecuadorean colleagues donned a very traditional Andean jacket one day, a so-called Otavalo jacket with figures of llamas handwoven throughout the fabric. He wore that symbol of his homeland proudly—until one of the Argentines mercilessly ridiculed the poor guy as if he were some country rube who strolled into a hip New York nightclub dressed in white sneakers, fanny pack, and striped polo shirt to find all the sophisticated locals sporting chic black.

The incident came to Fr. Bergoglio's attention; he simply invited the Argentine to wear that jacket for a week. In effect, the young Argentine Jesuit became a walking meditation for the whole community, a daily reminder to ponder that dignity involves acceptance of self for who one is, and character involves acceptance of others for who they are.

The New Leader: Start with Yourself

The content of Jesuit formation and the Spiritual Exercises are, of course, fundamentally Christian, but their "architecture" could not be more relevant as we try to develop ourselves, our children, students, or subordinates into the kinds of leaders we now need. Jesuits spend years in formation before the order unleashes them on the world, and much of that formation focuses not on acquiring the technical skills involved in teaching, preaching, or managing charitable institutions. It focuses on a more fundamental consideration: what does it mean to be human? And though the Spiritual Exercises ultimately aim to focus a Jesuit on following Jesus, their opening focus is oneself: look at yourself, your lived values, and your patterns of behavior.

Jesuits are learning habits of self-reflection that will endure and remain relevant through changing occupations and challenges. But they are also forging some core convictions. For Jesuits, those convictions are rooted in their religious beliefs. But, as it turns out, every leader must find his or her way to similar convictions in order to lead with integrity and character.

- I am flawed. I can't function effectively in the world if I give free rein to every impulse. I owe it to myself to battle my own demons.
- I am gifted and fundamentally good. There is a unique contribution I can make, and therefore,
- I am called to lead.

But called to lead for what end?

The next chapter focuses us on another vital set of convictions for the new leader. Yes, we have to commit to dig deep within ourselves in order to prepare ourselves to lead. But good leaders don't get stuck in their heads, needs, ambitions, or interests. Great leadership is always transcendent, and the new leader commits to transcend himself or herself, to rise above self and consider his or her relation to the wider world. Leaders have a worldview, not just a me-view, specifically: the world is not here to serve me; I am here to serve the world.

4

Washing Feet: Authentic Power Is Service

This is a symbol, it is a sign. . . . Washing feet means "I am at your service. . . ." As a priest and a bishop, I must be at your service.
—Pope Francis, Homily, March 28, 2013

You can't lead others if you can't lead yourself. But you can't lead others if you use power primarily to serve yourself and your ego. Leadership is not about you, it's about the rest of us—your family, community, colleagues, or customers.

"Get over yourself" is how we blunt New Yorkers put it. Pope Francis employs a richer concept: "Authentic power is service." The two phrases encapsulate a paradox of leadership. Leaders must dig deep within themselves, but that inward journey ultimately inspires them to leap beyond the shortsighted horizons that diminish so many leaders, who never see beyond my department, my company, my money, me, me, me.[52]

Good leaders see farther. They feel called to transcend themselves and serve a greater mission than self-interest alone.

What image can capture this ennobling nature of transcendent leadership?

What about Feet?

As Jesus and his disciples gathered for what turned out to be their Last Supper before his crucifixion, Jesus performed an utterly shocking gesture. "He poured water into a basin, and began to wash the disciples' feet," as the evangelist John recounts it. The disciple Peter protested, "You will never wash my feet," embarrassed and perhaps outraged that Jesus would perform work reserved for slaves, for non-Jewish slaves in fact, because such dirty work was considered beneath even a Jewish slave's dignity. But Jesus was making a point that had nothing to do with feet: "If I, your Lord and Teacher, have washed your feet, you also ought to wash one another's feet" (John 13:5, 14).

Movie and television portrayals of Jesus' life invariably depict this vivid vignette poorly. Jesus never breaks a sweat while laboring through a dozen pairs of feet that never seem in need of washing anyway, even though these disciples, sandaled at best and barefoot at worst, would have walked through a world without paved roads, pedicure shops, plumbing, or rigorous public-health standards. Jesus bathed filthy, dust-covered feet that might have been flecked with traces of human or animal waste. That's what Jesus did.

This iconic moment is commemorated in Christian churches on Holy Thursday, with selected parishioners standing in for the disciples and the parish priest for Jesus. The ritual typically unfolds like in the movies—that is, with no verisimilitude whatsoever. My brother was invited to have his foot washed when he was about ten years old, but my reverent Irish mother did the real washing, scrubbing away two or three epidermal layers, and, for good measure, dumping so much baby powder into my brother's shoe that a fragrant mushroom cloud wafted over the altar when he yanked off the shoe. The ritual is no less stylized when the pope enacts it at the Basilica of St. John Lateran, with select bishops or seminarians representing the apostles; I doubt any of them ever risked the career-ending gambit of presenting smelly feet to the pope.

But in 2013, Pope Francis recovered some of the shock value of Jesus' original gesture. He forsook St. John Lateran's gleaming marble floors for the drab stone flooring of the Casal del Marmo juvenile detention center, and he kissed the feet not of carefully chosen clerics and other Catholic worthies but of male and female juvenile delinquents who had been judged unworthy of walking the streets without close supervision.

Not everyone was impressed. Holy Thursday has multiple symbolic meanings within Catholicism, including as the institution of the priesthood, and some Catholics were affronted that a woman, much less a non-Christian, should be chosen to participate. One canon lawyer prissily tut-tutted what he called the pope's "questionable example."[53]

But the pope was doing what all good leaders sometimes do, jostling our imaginations when we become too complacent and stripping away the veneer of a familiar custom to expose the raw feel of a challenging truth. In this case, he was challenging our core assumptions about power, authority, and leadership. As he told the juveniles, "This is a symbol, it is a sign. . . . Washing feet means 'I am at your service. . . .' As a priest and a bishop, I must be at your service."[54]

But it was not only Church leaders he was challenging with that symbol. "Let us never forget that authentic power is service," he said elsewhere, addressing "all those who have positions of responsibility in economic, political, and social life, and all men and women of goodwill."[55]

Feet on the Ground, Every Day

Symbols and words count a lot, but what ultimately counts most are results. As presidential historian James MacGregor Burns once put it, "The ultimate test of practical leadership is the realization of intended, real change that meets people's enduring needs."[56] If stories about feet seem too esoteric, Burns focuses on a fundamental question that confronts every leader (and ought to haunt those who can't pass the test). Great leaders drive changes that meet people's enduring needs. So, is your leadership primarily serving people's needs or your own?

An emergency room doctor shows us what it looks like when the fundamental orientation to serve grips a leader's heart. Dr. David Hughes works at Mercy Medical Center in Durango, Colorado, part of one of the nation's largest health care systems, Catholic Health Initiatives (CHI), where I'm privileged to serve as board chair. "Reverence" is a core value; the book of Genesis says that humans are made in God's image and likeness.[57] (What would the world be like if we humans behaved as if we really believed that?) Well, our patients and colleagues will feel those words if we treat them reverently, aware that God is present in each of them.

That's a high standard for a workplace. After all, our employees struggle with the same intense demands that afflict every workplace: too much work, too much change at too rapid a pace, constant pressures to manage margins and expenses, and so on. I honor the great majority of our 85,000 employees who, despite these pressures, focus not only on the financial bottom line but on this ultimate bottom-line value that accounts for why we do what we do. Dr. Hughes is a case in point. A nurse, writing in one of our in-house publications, recalled a late-night emergency room visit from "one of our routine patients, who was without shoes. He was also homeless. When the patient was ready to be discharged, Dr. Hughes took off his shoes and gave them to the patient. The patient was appreciative, and Dr. Hughes left for home without shoes."[58]

After reading that story, I got in touch with Dr. Hughes. He instinctively deflected my comment that he had done something praiseworthy. "I really don't consider it a sacrifice at all. These shoes had put on many miles and I had run many races in them . . ." When the patient had said he needed shoes, "without much thought, I looked at my worn-out old running shoes, and handed them to the patient. I walked out of the ED and to my car and drove home, wearing only socks on my feet."

But why did you do it? I pressed. After all, it doesn't quite fit an ER doctor's job description. I was hoping to hear something about his deeper sense of purpose, and he didn't disappoint me. "As to my motivation to help people, I would have to say that it is part of a promise I made to God back when I was twelve. I am a member of the Church of Jesus Christ of Latter Day Saints and . . . it is my duty to act in [the Lord's] stead—basically doing what the Lord would do if he were in my place"—like, I suppose, giving your shoes to someone in need.

Dr. Hughes got back in touch with me the following day. He was apparently still discomfited that I had singled him out for praise, so he wanted to make sure I knew he was not exceptional. "In asking around amongst the staff in the emergency department, I was astounded to find out about many quiet selfless acts that occur on a regular basis, such as giving a patient a ride, helping someone out with $20, or just spending an extra moment to hear their story. One nurse who recently retired would ask any veteran about their stories from WWII."

One moral of that story: if you can get 85,000 health care workers, from neurosurgeons to janitors to accountants, so devoted to serving others that they would even offer their shoes if that's what it took, then most of the other outcomes you care so much about, like superb quality, safety, and patient care, will invariably follow. Dedication to serving others is the magic pill that makes for strong-performing, healthy organizations.

And that magic pill works not only in "helping" professions such as health care or social work. When my friend Ed Speed became chief executive of one of the nation's largest credit unions, he found what he describes as "a severely dysfunctional, self-protecting corporate culture . . . inward-focused, fearful, and often demeaning." (Many readers probably think Ed is describing their workplace, not his!) No business can excel when interactions with colleagues or customers are burdened by that mindset. Ed knew he had to flip that self-absorbed culture upside-down, and after some head-scratching, he and his management colleagues decided to use service as their lever to do so.

They started talking about it all the time and disseminated a new company-wide mantra: "If I am not directly serving a member [i.e., a customer], then I had better be 100% at the service of someone who is." In other words: everyone serves. Well, lots of companies bandy around pretty slogans and value statements, but we've become so jaded by corporate propaganda that we simply roll our eyes because words are so seldom matched by deeds. So Ed and his colleagues knew they had to hold each other highly accountable in order to turn nice-sounding words into reality: the management team committed to each other to be the prime role models of the behaviors they wanted, and every department got the chance twice a year to evaluate the service they were receiving from other departments. "It took slightly over four years to get traction," Ed recalls, but in time, the credit union was ranked one of Houston's top employers and started racking up customer-satisfaction results previously unrecorded in the industry.

But they got results not just because they put the right management and operational procedures in place, essential though those things are. They got results because they tapped into their employees' deepest convictions of why they were on earth—namely, to serve rather than be served. As Ed saw it, the "soil was prepared" for the service culture he wanted to instill through his employees' personal convictions. "I think that what we did was simply to create the environment where their faith life could be valued and expressed in service.

We did not add anything that the employees did not already possess within themselves. We just removed the barriers."

Such a culture of service inevitably influences everyone's behavior, including the way bosses relate to their teams. Not long after Fr. Bergoglio was appointed a bishop, one of his priests was hospitalized for an operation, and, as a fellow priest describes the incident: "[Bishop Bergoglio] spent the whole night at the hospital, concerned about the priest's health. *That really struck the rest of the clergy*, because they'd never seen an archbishop who spent the whole night in the hospital with one of them." [emphasis added][59] You can be sure that word of that incident spread more widely and impacted priests more profoundly than would any sermon about charity.

Fr. Tomás Bradley shares another story of a leader's undistracted focus on serving his subordinates. As provincial, Fr. Bergoglio had assigned a few Argentine seminarians to study in Japan, and some months later he made the thirty-five-hour, multiple-stop plane journey to check on their well-being. The young Jesuits, perhaps aware that Fr. Bergoglio had once hoped to be missioned to Japan himself, invited their superior on a short trip to see some of the tourist sites. The provincial's response? "I came here to see you." He devoted himself to one-on-one meetings with his seminarians, then headed back to the airport to begin the thirty-hour-plus journey back home.

Service at Personal Cost

Of course, sometimes the commitment to team can cost more than sleep or a sightseeing opportunity, as with Ethan Berman, my one-time J. P. Morgan colleague. After leaving Morgan, Ethan for some time was chief executive of Risk-Metrics, a highly specialized financial analysis firm. Specialists like RiskMetrics get paid lots of money to help firms assess their portfolio risks, which is why his 2004 memo to his board of directors mystified many. It had been a terrific year for the firm; Ethan had every reason to expect a lavish bonus from his board.

Then Ethan caused a problem of sorts. Not long before his board met to approve bonus payouts, Ethan wrote to inform them that "the firm's stronger than expected performance was driven by a large number of employees in other roles, and therefore I would like to see [them] paid greater bonuses than I receive."[60] Translation: I am the boss; we had a great year, but allocate to my subordinates some of what you would have paid me. If that concept doesn't astound, it should. Smart people are often drawn to this industry for the pay and nothing else; their identity and self-worth become wrapped up in how much they make relative to others.

But Ethan rejected that mentality and didn't want his pay to be determined solely by "what other executives at other similar companies are paid" as he wrote in his memo, because such approaches "are random and self-serving." By allocating to his team members money that otherwise would have filled his own pocket, Ethan made a powerful statement about serving one's team rather than oneself. What's more, he went on to affirm the same broad vision of leadership by asking his board to "broaden its definition of leaders" to include not just top bosses, but others who "display time and time again the values that we as a company believe in and therefore lead others by example not by mandate."[61] When we chatted, Ethan told me about the most gratifying part of the whole episode: numerous coworkers had sent his memo to their parents with pride. Not a bad barometer for leadership, come to think of it—will your coworkers and subordinates be proud to tell their parents about your style and values?

If Ethan's actions illustrate one vision of leadership, the chief executive of Viacom, which brings us MTV and Comedy Central, exemplified close to the opposite. Three weeks before Christmas in 2008, the company's two top executives penned a memo to staff, but it didn't exactly brim with Yuletide cheer or Comedy Central-style chuckles. That year had been horrific in world markets; Viacom's stock price had been halved, and the company carried a heavy debt load. Its long-term health, the executives wrote, "will depend on our shared commitment to adapt . . . and to make difficult choices." They needed a cost structure more in step "with the evolving economic environment," so they announced that 7 percent of the workforce, more than eight hundred employees, would have to be terminated, and salaries would be frozen for all senior-level managers.[62]

I understand the "difficult choices" these leaders made: when markets nosedive, companies may die if managements shrink from painful measures like layoffs. I had to do the same more than once over the years. It's always agonizing but sometimes unavoidable.

Still, we might respectfully ask if these executives could have made at least one more "difficult choice" that would have embodied the "shared commitment" their memo extolled: perhaps Viacom's chief executive could have declined, Ethan Berman-style, at least a tiny bit of the $23 million pay package the board had awarded him for that same dismal year of 2008, when hundreds of subordinates looked forward to pink slips while he looked forward to a $3 million increase over his previous year's pay package.[63]

Few of us will become corporate chief executives. We won't confront the question "how much pay is enough," but a more fundamental one: will I go through life primarily to serve myself or to serve others? Our answer—our conviction about human purpose and the role of a leader—will determine our behaviors as parents, teachers, entry-level employees, or managers. And our commitments and behavior patterns are unlikely to change dramatically over time; people don't get older, as the saying goes—they just become more so. When self-serving mid-level managers climb all the way to the executive suite, they typically don't morph into chief executives who understand themselves as serving subordinates, customers, and the broader community. Their me-first ambition and careerism have by then become too deeply ingrained and reinforced by a successful rise to the top.

The new leader has to find within himself or herself the strength to resist the poisonous pull of the me-first culture, inside and outside workplaces and organizations. That's why our most important leadership formation is the personal, too often-neglected inner work of forging the convictions today that will guide our behavior tomorrow, like making the commitment to serve.

Formation for a Service Mentality

Ignatius of Loyola understood that. He designed Jesuit training accordingly. Novices such as the future Pope Francis were (and are) confronted with a stark choice during the thirty-day Spiritual Exercises that emerge once more as the key crucible of Jesuit leadership formation. Not long after the self-assessment meditations profiled in the previous chapter, Ignatius has Jesuits imagine the world as a battlefield, pitting the followers of Jesus against those of Lucifer, who is "seated on a throne of fire and smoke, in aspect horrible and terrifying."[64] Ignatius's late medieval imagery always seems over the top, but give credit where due: he certainly mastered a Hollywood-ready flair for cinematic depiction!

"The enemy of human nature,"[65] as Ignatius calls the force of evil in our lives, specializes in self-destructive "snares and chains" that pervert our perspective on the world and our role in it. Snares and chains? As Ignatius sees it, we pursue money, power, or honor, but once we grasp them, they end up controlling us, shackling us, if you will. The fifty or so of us trainees who started J. P. Morgan's management-training program were a happy-go-lucky crowd who had charmed lives: doing interesting work for good pay at a well-respected company.

But over time, the dark undertow of greed and ambition became hard to resist: my bonus seemed incredibly generous until I found out a half hour later that a colleague received a bigger one; I congratulated (but more so envied) the colleague who became a vice president six months before I did or who was promoted more quickly up the ranks. The first innocent steps onto a career path can become a slippery slope toward an addiction to what Ignatius called "vain honor from the world, and finally to surging pride."[66] Under such subtle but relentless forces, my world begins to revolve around me, what I earn, and what others think of me. That's how the enemy of human nature works.

Ignatius warns his trainees against this trap of self-absorption, inviting Jesuits to be humble rather than honor-obsessed, simple rather than money-obsessed, and focused on serving others (as companions of Jesus) rather than self-obsessed. Ignatius hammers home this fundamental choice in the Exercises and enshrines it as the cornerstone of Jesuit culture. The Jesuit motto is *Ad maiorem Dei gloriam*, "for the greater glory of God," which inspires a forever-restless, almost quixotic energy: let me pursue not only what is for God's glory but always seek what might be for God's even greater glory.

But at the same moment, that motto implicitly challenges a Jesuit's every thought and action, as if to say, "Hey Jesuit, that eloquent sermon you are crafting, or that new university building project that you are envisioning—are you doing that only for God's glory, or are you serving yourself and stroking your ego?"

When I was an eighteen-year-old Jesuit-in-training, Ignatius's extravagantly Baroque depiction of Lucifer's fiery throne struck me as pretty outdated; in fact, that stuff about "vain honor" and "surging pride" seemed pretty old-fashioned too.

The problem was not that I was too sophisticated for Ignatius but too naïve to appreciate what reality is like. A dozen years in investment banking made clear that the "enemy of human nature," whether one understands that idea in religious or purely psychological terms, absolutely exists. Greed, pride, arrogance, envy, self-absorption, vanity, and a dozen other personal demons can distort our perspective until they dominate us.

Adult life does sometimes seem like a spiritual battlefield, a struggle between self-absorption and a lived commitment to some purpose greater than self. That everyday struggle typically plays out in the subtlest ways, as we decide whether to devote the next free hour to television or to our children, or a few extra dollars to yet another new shirt or to charity. And as one's leadership platform becomes more prominent, the temptations rise commensurately.

Why We All Must Think Like Leaders

We risk trouble if we presume that this struggle concerns only celebrities, millionaire executives, or high-profile politicians. Pope Francis, for example, as a good son of Ignatius, appreciates that every human person is subject to the lure of overweening self-interest, even those who have chosen the simplest, noblest lines of work, like his fellow priests and church workers. Though their calling hardly offers the allure of fame or riches, the pope sees the demons of clericalism and careerism at work. "These social climbers exist even in the Christian communities, no? Those people who are looking out for themselves . . . They want glory for themselves . . ."[67]

Nor is a pope himself immune to the same pitfalls. In fact, weekly megadoses of public adulation at papal audiences may render the pontiff even more susceptible than the rest of us to those Ignatian-named demons of honor and pride. The Jesuit pope surely knows that, which is why he wrote the Argentine bishops for prayers, that "I do not grow proud and always know how to listen to what God wants and not what I want."[68]

In fact, not a week seems to go by when Pope Francis does not mention the struggle for humility, occasionally referencing his spiritual father Ignatius's stark imagery of a spiritual battleground. It's not that he's saddled with out-moded, medieval ways of thinking; rather, he sees that the battle to keep ego in check has become even harder in the here and now. Consider what we now have to cope with. Leading politicians, businesspeople, or televangelists not only become media rock stars, but many of them earn annually what a teacher, civil servant, or lower-ranking functionary in a company might earn over 300 years. Chief executives are annually ranked by pay in national news magazines. So are the world's richest people, and so are the best colleges and the biggest college endowments. In fact, just about anyone with a determined drive for fame can find at least passing celebrity if willing to flaunt his or her dysfunction on reality television.

The incentives to self-interested success are many and public; the incentives to service of others can be few, often no more than the leader's personal commitment.

Authentic Power Is Service

This chapter has focused on the question that confronts every leader: are you here to serve yourself or the rest of us? The new leader's answer is to transcend self and rise above what Pope Francis called the "many small or great idols that we have and in which we take refuge, on which we often seek to base our security. They are idols that we sometimes keep well hidden; they can be ambition, careerism, a taste for success, placing ourselves at the centre, the tendency to dominate others, the claim to be the sole masters of our lives, some sins to which we are bound, and many others. . . . I would like a question to resound in the heart of each one of you, and I would like you to answer it honestly: Have I considered which idol lies hidden in my life . . .?"[69]

The language of "idols" may seem musty and hyper-religious but in fact could not be more apt. To be sure, self-interest has its place: I worked in a global financial firm long enough to appreciate the truth of Adam Smith's observation: "It is not from the benevolence of the butcher, the brewer, or the baker that we expect our dinner, but from their regard to their own interest."[70] I've seen first-hand in Asia whole societies lifted up, prosperity blossom, jobs created, and human dignity flourish simply because energetic—and, yes, self-interested—people got the chance to use their talents creatively and productively.

But I've also seen what happens when unchecked ambition, careerism, and self-interest run absolutely amuck, leaving us with intractable and worsening problems—in business, politics, civic life, and religious life. These problems won't be solved by self-focused leaders, but only by those who can lift their horizons and see farther, transcending the same old narrow categories of me, my department, my paycheck, my political allies, my religion, or whatever it may be.

The new leader will sweep away the idols of self-interest and lead us toward what serves the common good, what respects all people's rights and freedoms, and what protects our beloved children, and their children after them.

Still, though the new leader's vision transcends the horizon of self, the leader must also keep his or her feet planted on the ground—as the next chapter explores—squarely in the muck of everyday reality.

5

Dusty Shoes: Immerse Yourself in the World's Joys and Sufferings

[U]nless we train ministers capable of warming people's hearts, of walking with them in the night, of dialoguing with their hopes and disappointments, of mending their brokenness, what hope can we have for our present and future journey?
—Pope Francis, Address to Brazilian Bishops, July 27, 2013

Pope Francis passed over the footwear that has long been famously associated with popes: red shoes. Etched in Fr. Hernán Paredes's memory is an image of Fr. Bergoglio in footwear that has never been associated with popes: plastic farm boots.

Paredes studied at the Jesuit's Colegio Máximo San José. Remember that long Jesuit training process described in earlier chapters? Well, because Jesuits are in formation for so long, sometimes there are lots of trainees. During the mid-1980s, Hernán was one of seventy-plus trainees at a sprawling Buenos Aires seminary complex, where some studied philosophy, others humanities, and still others theology.

Fr. Bergoglio was their boss, the rector, a post he had assumed after finishing his stint as provincial of Argentina's Jesuits in 1979. Before focusing on Bergoglio's footwear, it's worth focusing on how he wound up in that job, which shows how Ignatius of Loyola's organizational-design instincts challenge the conventions of today's supposedly enlightened corporations. Bergoglio had been the boss of all Argentina's Jesuits, and when his six-year term ended, his successor assigned him to a new post: shepherding that mob of trainees.

He *stepped down*, and his successor assigned him his new job. Consider, in contrast, how contemporary companies typically manage transitions. We pride ourselves on crafting elaborate succession plans for senior managers but rarely implement them; most senior managers are less often "succeeded" than ousted or overthrown, sometimes gracefully but more often ignominiously. They don't step down as Bergoglio did; rather, we find their fingernail tracks in the carpet after they have been dragged from office, multimillion-dollar golden parachutes sometimes trailing behind them.

The Danger of Unchecked Ambition

Ignatius of Loyola might suggest that we handle managerial transitions poorly because we are enslaved to status, ego, or personal insecurities. No manager who rotates out of a senior position, for example, will agree to soldier on in a lesser role; it would be beneath his or her dignity. And, anyway, no new senior manager wants his predecessor to hang around. Eager to place his own stamp on the organization and paranoid that a predecessor might undermine his authority and plot a return to power, the new boss doesn't only usher his predecessor into oblivion but, for good measure, exiles the old boss's protégés in order to install his own loyal palace guard (loyal, that is, until one of them sees his own chance to vault ahead by dethroning the king).

Ignatius of Loyola was terrified that unchecked ambition could wreck his Jesuits. If you gather talented people, after all, it's natural for them to want to compete, so the trick is to channel ambition and energy toward mission and away from infighting. Ignatius crafted his organizational structure with that in mind. His Jesuit rule book—*Constitutions*—pronounces overweening ambition "the mother of all evils in any community or congregation"[71] and mandates Jesuits report colleagues suspected of scheming for higher office. What's more, Ignatius mandated fixed terms for virtually every managerial job in the Jesuits, save that of their global head, in order to assure that even a high-profile managerial job within the Jesuits would remain, well, just a job. No one had to oust Bergoglio, because he had to step down after a fixed term. Nor did he get to pick a plum next posting for himself or demand a golden parachute because it was his successor's prerogative to decide Bergoglio's next posting. For Jesuits who grow a bit too fond of being a boss, that wait for reassignment can be a cold shower of renewed humility.

That Bergoglio was assigned to oversee trainees highlights another provocative aspect of Jesuit organizational philosophy. A corporate take on that assignment would be: "This guy had become one of the company's top 200 global executives by age thirty-nine, and now he is going to supervise trainees? Ouch. Career over." Ignatius would see things differently: you succeed only by fielding committed, high-quality professionals, and you get them only when your new recruits are molded by committed, high-quality leaders. So the Jesuit trainee-formation job is typically entrusted not to a safe if unspectacular pair of hands but to a role model who might inspire.

Such a career path, not to mention the long Jesuit formation process itself, may seem odd and outdated. That's because we've forgotten what A. G. Lafley, Procter & Gamble's legendarily successful chief executive, called his "most enduring" role, to "develop leaders who not only can lead and inspire change themselves but, even more importantly, are capable of building other leaders. . . . Nothing I do will have a greater impact on the long-term health [of the company]."[72] Or of a family, school, or any other organization for that matter. But leadership formation takes time and effort. We're too seldom willing to bear that burden: it's far easier to train someone in a few job skills than make the serious commitment required to form that person as a leader.

So we take short cuts, ignoring the plain fact that Pope Francis could not conceivably be the leader he is today without his long, intensive formation over the years. Jesuits still willingly make that commitment, so Fr. Bergoglio's career path, from boss to formation head, would make complete sense in their way of looking at the world. So too would the unlikely career path of my Jesuit friend John Fitzgibbons. After earning a PhD in English literature, he began teaching in a Jesuit university, compiling administrative experience, and even rising to serve on the governing board of two universities.

Then he was yanked from university life and put in charge of a Jesuit novitiate, trading a university board seat for oversight of twenty trainees. That sounds like a career derailment, as does Bergoglio's apparent come-down, from boss of Argentina's Jesuits to supervision of a few dozen. But Jesuits are not trained to think in terms of "derailment" and careerism (at least, the good ones don't; I've known one or two who seemed to like having prestigious jobs).

The pope would have a word or two for the careerists. In fact, he *has* had a word or two for them. He addressed the Pontifical Ecclesiastical Academy, which trains the priest-diplomats who end up hobnobbing with the world's ambassadors, and, frequently enough, rise through the Church hierarchy themselves to become bishops or higher. The pope warned them not to let their prestigious work go to their heads: "Careerism is leprosy! Leprosy!" he stressed. Priests had to labor only for the "cause of the Gospel and the fulfillment of the mission," and never for "public recognition."[73]

That's not to say a mission-oriented leader always has to be thrilled with what he's asked to do on behalf of the organization. John Fitzgibbons, the university board member who became novice director, put it to me plainly: "I really did not want to be novice director, but I knew the Society had a right to call me to serve."

And then he put it into a deeper perspective. When his Jesuit boss assigned him to manage trainees, "my heartfelt response was that doing formation work is an honor and a privilege, even if I wasn't trained for it. For me, it was an act of obedience as well; I trusted this was God's will and that even if I didn't deeply desire to do this kind of ministry [Jesuit formation work] it was holy work."

As it turns out, a few years and a few postings later, Fitzgibbons, one-time master of twenty novices, was named president of Regis University, which enrolls some 15,000 on-campus and online students, one of the largest student populations of any Jesuit university. Those kinds of career trajectories, virtually unthinkable in corporate life, become possible when team members are willing to focus less on status than on mission: one-time bosses willingly step aside to become field soldiers again, their performance enhanced by their management experience, and vice versa.

As for Fr. Bergoglio, as the world now knows, his stint supervising a Jesuit seminary didn't seem to derail his long-term trajectory either. And his leadership style in that seminary embodies the leadership paradox we explore in this chapter and next: great leaders commit to immerse themselves in the day-to-day world, yet also withdraw from the world. They are reflective people who step back to find serenity, balance, and perspective, as the following chapter will elaborate. They engage the everyday relentlessly yet transcend the everyday; fully immersed in the world, they are not completely "of" it; worldly, they are likewise spiritual.

Those Argentine seminarians had their heads soaring while pondering Aristotle and Thomas Aquinas, but Fr. Bergoglio made sure they were thoroughly grounded. In fact, not only grounded but plenty dirty: the Colegio Máximo complex incorporated a farm. The produce helped support the financially straitened Jesuit community. I asked Hernán Paredes what animals they kept, and his precise answer, a quarter century after his time there, convinced me that I could rely on this guy's memory: "Our animals?" He started rattling off a census. "We used to have 120 pigs, 53 sheep, 180 rabbits, we had cows—that's where we got our milk . . ." Who tended the farm? "Well," Paredes continues, "there were a couple of Jesuit brothers who were experts in managing the farm, and that was their main job. But, all of us, we would work on the farm in some way or another, some of us more than others. Bergoglio, too," Paredes adds, "He worked. I have in my mind an image, one afternoon when I was coming back from the parish where I was helping, seeing him there in his plastic boots, feeding the pigs."

Think of those work boots as leadership footwear, a way of saying: I won't ask you to do anything that I'm unwilling to do myself. But Fr. Bergoglio's dirty-footed leadership had even more profound meaning, as Sr. María Soledad Albisú will help us understand. She occasionally visited Bergoglio during those same years for spiritual direction, what the secular world might call "advanced life coaching." Ignatius of Loyola insisted that every Jesuit regularly consult a spiritual director, and Fr. Bergoglio apparently was a popular one: Paredes tells me that a few dozen of his fellow trainees consulted him.

The previous chapter helps pinpoint just why Ignatius thought the director relationship invaluable. We humans have blind spots and are clever enough to rationalize even our most dysfunctional behaviors; a trusted mentor can help us recognize and confront our rationalizations. And all of us must face major life decisions. Discerning the best path forward can be frustrating—reasons for and against each prospective course of action can run around our heads in confusing circles. A wise guide can help us wrestle our motives into some intelligible pattern and help us hold ourselves accountable against the values we profess.

God Found Among the Lowliest Things

Fr. Bergoglio played that role as Soledad Albisú, then a layperson, contemplated a religious vocation. But as they chatted informally before or after those sessions, Bergoglio the spiritual director also shared some leadership theory, not that he would have called it that. In a short piece published in *The Tablet*, Albisú recalls him showing her around the community farm. "He took me outside where the community kept sheep and pigs. He told me that this was a good place to pray and to remember that God is to be found in the lowliest things."[74]

She also recalls that Fr. Bergoglio "always insisted that the seminarians should go out at the weekends to the poor barrios to offer [religious instruction] to the children. He said that someone who is able to make the catechism simple enough for a child to understand is a wise person." And when the seminarians returned from the barrio, he "would look to see if they had dusty feet. If they came back with clean feet, he took it as a sign that they'd done nothing."

Hernán Paredes can vouch for that. He visited Cardinal Bergoglio in Buenos Aires many years after his seminary days, less than two years before the cardinal was elected pope. Paredes was by then working in New York, teaching in a Jesuit high school on weekdays and on Sundays celebrating Mass for Hispanic communities across the city. Cardinal Bergoglio, for his part, was preparing for retirement; upon reaching age seventy-five, Catholic bishops are mandatorily required to resign from their postings. Bergoglio had submitted his resignation letter and was waiting for Pope Benedict to accept it. (Sometimes life has other plans in store.)

As they chatted, Paredes recounted that he had visited an impoverished district not far from the old seminary, where Bergoglio used to send the trainees each weekend to teach catechism to little children. Cardinal Bergoglio feigned an inspection of Paredes's shoes and then laughed. "You visited the barrio? You must have gotten your feet dirty!"

"Yes," Hernán said, laughing, "very dirty—just like the old days."

Those dirty feet—Bergoglio's at the pig trough and the seminarian's in the barrio—crystallize a vital but increasingly endangered leadership habit: the commitment to stay in touch, deal with reality, accept accountability for one's work and decisions, and recognize that we humans are all inextricably linked—both in our local community and globally. Many of us in leadership positions are too easily "disintermediated"—cut off, alienated, insulated—from reality on the ground. We might manage dozens of people but know little about their personal lives and struggles. Or, like last chapter's Viacom executives, we look at financial statements, stock prices, projected income streams, and competitor strategies before concluding that shareholder value is best served by a thousand-person downsizing. About the only place we didn't look during that whole decision process and its aftermath? Into the face of the 750th or 751st person who lost his or her job. Good leaders are in touch, relentlessly in touch with the world's joys and sufferings, and aware that in an interconnected world, one person's decisions often affect the lives of many unseen others.

Technology can exacerbate dehumanization, not only because it accelerates work's pace, scale, and complexity, but also because it invites us to insulate ourselves from life's grittiness. Yes, we may be virtually connected to "friends" all over the world through social media, but our living connection to reality can suffer as a result. We can choose to be in touch with only the reality we want and may gradually fall out of touch with the reality we do not wish to engage. A *New York Times* guest columnist mused disconcertedly over "smart" contact lenses that might soon allow us to stroll down the street and alter the reality before us, "mak[ing] homeless people disappear from view," for example. (Why let a downer like a homeless vagrant spoil a window-shopping stroll on a beautiful spring afternoon?)[75] A Samsung advertising campaign for a digital television line has inadvertently provided a slogan for this whole disintermediated era: "Reality. What a letdown."[76] In fact, we don't even need smart contact lenses to erase the homeless from sight. It has happened already. Pope Francis has observed " . . . that some homeless people die of cold on the streets is not news. In contrast, a ten point drop on the stock markets of some cities, is a tragedy. A person dying is not news, but if the stock markets drop ten points it is a tragedy! Thus people are disposed of, as if they were trash."[77]

What we might call the "alternate reality syndrome" gets worse the higher we climb. Jeff Sonnenfeld of the Yale School of Management laments that today's chief executives "are more insulated and pampered and elevated than any before."[78] When things go wrong, they abjure accountability for frauds or missteps perpetrated by key lieutenants because they "didn't know" what was happening one or two layers down in the organization. It's not "the buck stops here" for these proudly out-of-touch CEOs, it's more like, "let me preserve plausible denial for the buck possibly stopping here." That's why we need leaders willing to struggle against the alternate reality syndrome. Kudos to Pope Francis for waging his own little rebellion; he has refused to be cocooned in his papal apartment and insulated from day-to-day reality by a bubble of monsignori, Swiss guards, and other functionaries. Instead, he has settled into the Vatican guesthouse, in part to live as simple and poor a lifestyle as might realistically be permitted a pope, but also to rub shoulders and share meals with anyone else sitting down in the guesthouse cafeteria.

The choice of simpler quarters may have been a shocking departure from papal tradition but was completely consistent with Pope Francis's history—he had similarly eschewed Buenos Aires's episcopal palace for a humble apartment. In fact, the choice of living quarters reflects Pope Francis's more fundamental preoccupation with remaining in touch, and it's worth looking at this preoccupation through a leadership lens: what does the leader and his team gain from "dirty footed" leadership?

Do the Laundry and Inspire the Team

Fr. Tomás Bradley arrived at the Colegio Máximo in 1985, just after finishing his novitiate and pronouncing vows of poverty, chastity, and obedience. I asked for his recollections of Fr. Bergoglio during that time, and here's how he started: "Jorge [the way he referred to Jorge Bergoglio] was the rector and also the 'laundry man' of the house." Fr. Tomás remembers Bergoglio "already at 5:30 in the morning, he would be placing clothes into those two industrial washing machines we had." And there were lots of clothes, apparently: "There were more than a hundred of us living in that place," he adds.

Enough, already, some readers are surely thinking. *We get it: the man who is now the pope was humble enough to feed pigs and do the laundry when he ran a seminary. So what?* We might also be thinking, *If I had entrusted the care of seminarians to the guy, I would prefer that he use his professional expertise to form future leaders and priests, not waste time doing the laundry.*

That's just it: he *was* forming leaders and priests. Look at it this way: Hernán Paredes and Tomás Bradley must have seen Bergoglio do and say thousands of things—why do pig feeding and laundry washing stand out as indelible memories?

Anyone who has worked for a good leader knows the answer: few things cement our loyalty like knowing the boss is no prima donna but part of the team, someone who won't just ask us to sacrifice for others but will also do so herself. That's why, for example, Marine officers always line up at the back of the mess line, behind the men and women under their command. They are sending an important leadership message: if ever there is not enough food for everyone, I will starve before I let you starve.

I recall one of my own missed chances at "laundry man"-style team leadership. A clerical team that worked for a subordinate of mine once had to sacrifice a Saturday morning to stuff envelopes, print and organize hundreds of compensation letters, or accomplish some other labor-intensive administrative exercise. The Friday afternoon before their mind-numbing waste of a spring weekend morning, I happened to be chatting with their boss about his and my respective weekend plans. I forget mine but will always remember his: he would surprise his clerical team that Saturday morning with some coffee and pastries and spend an hour or so working beside them.

None of them would have expected me to show up because I was their boss's boss. But none of them expected him to show up either, just as I presume those young Jesuit seminarians did not expect Bergoglio to do his share of the grunt work.

That's the point, of course. No one remembers the leader who merely does the expected, like giving rah-rah pep talks about being part of the team, but everyone remembers the leader who gets her hands dirty alongside us to prove we are all one team.

Finding Answers and Solidarity: The Smell of the Sheep

But there's even more to it than building team loyalty, and another of my leadership missteps helps introduce yet another benefit of hands-dirty management. For a while, I and other managing directors were overseeing the consolidation of operations from various European locations into one central geographic hub. It was confusing, difficult work, what we colloquially called an utter dog's breakfast of a job. None of us managing directors could easily engineer the consolidation for our particular areas of oversight. One of them poked his head in my office as I was scrutinizing some spreadsheet and asked what headway I was making with the workflow re-engineering project. Not much, I confessed. He offered these parting words before moving on, "Well, you're not going to find the answer sitting behind that desk." His comment stung because he was right: I was essentially hiding behind my desk. The answers weren't in a report; they were out among my team and the work, scrutinizing the process firsthand, side by side with my team and brainstorming solutions together.

Fr. Bergoglio seems to have intuitively understood that lesson I had to learn; namely, leaders must insert themselves into the thick of problems and opportunities. Another episode from his seminary-management days makes clear. As Jesuit Fr. Alejandro Gauffin related in a personal interview, the bishop of Buenos Aires decided to launch a new parish in the vicinity of the Jesuit seminary and asked Fr. Bergoglio to serve as its first pastor (apparently because he had so much free time remaining after feeding pigs, doing laundry, serving as spiritual director for a few dozen Jesuits, teaching theology, and who knows what else).

This would be Fr. Bergoglio's first concentrated experience in parish work, and his approach proved unconventional. Non-Catholic readers may not know how Catholic churches typically "market" themselves, so a short if irreverent primer may help: they open the doors, publish a Mass schedule (sometimes where the general public can see it, but not always), and then wait for people to show up. That's it. Not exactly what one would call scrappy or creative. The pope seems intent on changing the passive "build it and they will come model" because, frankly and with all due respect, "they" are no longer coming in many parts of the world, at least not in the numbers of generations ago, when "cradle to grave" Catholicism was culturally common.

As Fr. Gauffin recalls it, that new parish was inaugurated on a March 19, the feast of St. Joseph in the Catholic liturgical calendar, which presents a delicious coincidence: it's exactly the same feast day as Pope Francis's 2013 inauguration as head of his marginally larger parish, the global Church. There are one or two differences, of course: the global parish church, for example, is St. Peter's Basilica, handiwork of Bernini, Michelangelo, and a few others; the Buenos Aires church was a converted shed, handiwork of whoever had some spare plywood.

No matter. As Bergoglio saw it then and sees it now, a lot of the action takes place outside the walls anyway. He drew up a crude map of the neighborhood, sectioned it off into small zones, and assigned seminarian volunteers like Gauffin to each zone. To do what? Get their feet dirty. Walk the streets. Meet people where they live. Here's how Gauffin put it: "The slogans I remember most were these, 'get into the neighborhood and walk it,' 'don't "comb the sheep," meet all of them,' 'visit the poor and take care of their needs,' 'get the kids for [religious instruction].'" In other words, "You're not going to find your answer sitting behind that desk." In fact, now as Pope Francis, he is reinforcing exactly the same ideas, telling bishops assembled in Brazil that "we need a Church capable of walking at people's side, of doing more than simply listening to them; a Church which accompanies them on their journey."[79]

But even when you do encounter reality face-to-face instead of through a computer keyboard, the answers don't come immediately. Rather, more problems surface, and, almost invariably, the problems seem more varied, complex, and vivid than they seemed from the safe perch of a workstation. Gauffin continues his story: "The '80s were tough in Argentina." Well, even I knew that, reading about the country's economic crisis in the *New York Times* while sipping coffee on my air-conditioned train commute to Wall Street. But Fr. Bergoglio and his colleagues weren't reading about it; they were visiting neighborhood families that could provide their kids only one daily meal. Gauffin remembers Bergoglio saying something like, "We can't sit around with our arms crossed while people are hungry and we [here in the seminary] lack nothing."

But what to do? He was a religious superior trying to launch a parish; his seminarian colleagues were philosophy students, not social workers. Well, maybe philosophy came in handy. The philosophical brainteaser known as Zeno's Paradox is not worth recounting here, but its punch line is relevant: *solvitur ambulando*, that is, "it is solved by walking." Sometimes you just start. You grasp the full dimensions of the problem only by wading into its midst, and the way forward becomes clear only by taking some initiative, any initiative; that first step generates momentum for the second, and the second gives you enough perspective to see whether you're heading in the right direction. To get themselves started, as Gauffin puts it, "We got a big cooking pot and some volunteers" and they started distributing meals, first working out of a woman parishioner's house, then putting their feeding station "in a large field . . . under a tarp . . . and [we] lit a cooking fire there." Eventually the ramshackle effort spawned a broader community-service program, now housed in its own building, the Casa del Niño San José.

And the parish? That was the original mandate, after all, not social work. Well, the parish grew, so quickly that it has since been subdivided more than once. At least three parishes or chapels now serve that neighborhood.

Walk the neighborhood, see what the needs are, try to do something, and "Don't comb the sheep," Bergoglio warned them. Every culture has its own version of that concept. "Don't skim the cream": don't lazily content yourself with the rich froth that floats to the surface. "Don't cherry pick"—get in there and meet everyone, including those who don't want to see you. Though Fr. Bergoglio was a city boy, he evidently likes his sheep imagery. A few days after his papal election, he preached the Holy Thursday Chrism Mass, which commemorates the Catholic priesthood's establishment. Dozens of clerics gathered in St. John Lateran's ornate basilica for the once-in-a-lifetime moment: a brand new pope's first formal sermon to his priests. Some, sitting in finely starched vestments, may have anticipated sophisticated theological analysis from this pope who had not only completed the extensive course of Jesuit studies but also spent time in Germany pursuing a doctorate in theology.

Instead, they heard about sheep smell.

He exhorted them to be good shepherds, so deeply inserted "in the midst of their flock" that they were "living with the smell of the sheep." He recalled the biblical anointing of Aaron the high priest and told the clerics that their own priestly anointing "is not intended just to make us fragrant, much less to be kept in a jar, for then it would become rancid . . . and the heart bitter." He told them to "go out of themselves" to the "outskirts where there is suffering" instead of hanging back and becoming merely "intermediaries, managers," the sort of priest who "never puts his own skin and his own heart on the line."[80]

Pope Francis has since come back to the same ideas multiple times, often in equally vivid imagery: "A Church that does not go out of itself, sooner or later, sickens from the stale air of closed rooms," or "We understand reality better not from the center, but from the outskirts," or, perhaps most sharply, "We cannot become starched Christians, too polite, who speak of theology calmly over tea. We have to become courageous Christians and seek out those who need help most."[81]

Yes, be courageous and seek out those who most need help, but not with the condescendingly smug attitude that you have so much to give these benighted, inferior creatures. In fact, the "courage" called for includes the willingness to admit how little you really understand of the world and must learn from the poor, as Fr. Bergoglio made abundantly clear to his seminarians. Fr. Tomás Bradley remembers Bergoglio instructing them that "You are going to learn from the people before you teach them anything." Precisely because the seminarians had so much to learn, Fr. Bergoglio used to tell them that closeness to poor people was "important for the formation of a priest's heart."

Dirty-Footed Leadership: Some Lessons Learned

What can leaders and would-be leaders make of all this? Catholic pastors might sit up, note their pontiff's work in the trenches, and take a page from his playbook as today's Church attempts to reengage the many millions of Catholics who have drifted away. But what about the rest of us? We're not running churches, after all; we're running businesses or schools. Many of us don't share the pope's religious tradition.

To be sure, the pope's efforts are inextricably intertwined with his broader Catholic vision: he constantly exhorts Catholics to engage the world and especially the neediest, but he just as constantly cautions that the Church is not simply an NGO; all its efforts must flow from its holistic religious mission.[82]

But we can nonetheless extract wisdom relevant to any walk of life:

- *You can't lead us if you don't know our reality.* To win credibility and allegiance, you can't merely know about our lives but have to know our lives and identify with our challenges, like the Fr. Bergoglio who knew the reality of starting household chores at 5:30 a.m. or who saw what hunger looked like in his community instead of merely reading about it. Hernán Paredes recalls a telling moment from those seminary days, when Fr. Bergoglio pointed out a statue of Our Lady of Sorrows and made a comment like, "You know, the older I get, the more I relate to Our Lady of Sorrows." That is, the longer you walk the world's streets with your eyes open, the more suffering you see, and conscientious people can't help but be burdened by the sufferings of fellow humans. *Solidarity* is the fancy term for this sensibility of compassionate unity that the poet John Donne captures: "any man's death diminishes me, because I am involved in mankind, and therefore never send to know for whom the bell tolls; it tolls for thee."
- *You will know our reality only by walking among us.* Get out from behind the desk, remove the "smart contact lenses" that blot unpleasantness from sight, and look around. Go to the outskirts, get your feet dirty, get the smell of the sheep on yourself.
- *Don't just look; do something.* Once you walk among us and know our reality, you will never be content to witness suffering passively.
- *Do something and learn something.* You have something unique to offer (remember chapter 3's key theme), but you probably have more to gain. As Fr. Bergoglio reminded his seminarians, you're going to learn from people before you teach them anything.

And the pope's warning to his own Church is true for any other business or organization I've ever worked with: "A Church that does not go out of itself, sooner or later, sickens from the stale air of closed rooms." As soon as you lose touch with reality on the ground and the perspectives of those you "theoretically" serve, you are lost. The pope put it this way to his Church, and we can all make the relevant analogies to our own lives: "Theoretical poverty doesn't do anything. Poverty is learned by touching the flesh of the poor Christ in the humble, the poor."[83] Along these lines, Francis posed two questions to one audience: "Tell me, when you give alms, do you look the person in the eye? . . . [D]o you touch the hand of the person you are giving them to or do you toss the coin at him or her?"[84]

At the Core of Pope Francis's Leadership

But it would shortchange Francis to lay out these behaviors without also elaborating the worldview that drives them, as if leadership were merely tactics. This book's premise is that leaders act on beliefs and convictions formed long before they reached the executive suite or papal apartments. So what drives Pope Francis's commitment to immersion in the world? That habit, like many others, bears the fingerprints of his Jesuit formation, specifically the worldview that he imbibed from Ignatius's Spiritual Exercises. And as following paragraphs explore more of Ignatius's worldview, readers are invited to ponder and sharpen their own convictions.

Previous chapters have gradually pieced together a distinctly Ignatian worldview. Commit to know yourself deeply, including your frailties, and come to some peaceful acceptance of yourself and your calling to lead. Then, commit to "get over yourself" to serve a purpose greater than the self, to labor for God's greater glory. No surprise that the full title of Ignatius's program of meditation is "Spiritual Exercises, to overcome oneself and to order one's life."[85]

Self-mastery doesn't always come easily, and Ignatius used the vivid imagery of life as a spiritual battlefield, where the enemy of human nature strives to undermine us from the call to great purpose. We might suppose, therefore, that Ignatius must have regarded the world—where this battle for our allegiance plays out—as a grim place, fraught with pitfalls and temptations. Surely anyone intent on a heavenly reward would be wise to limit engagement with this perilous world, where the enemy of human nature lurks around every corner.

Actually, Ignatius believed the opposite.

Don't withdraw; plunge in. The world is not a bad place, but an unfathomably good place. God created it, and what God made is good by definition. In the Spiritual Exercises' pinnacle meditation, Ignatius counsels us to, "consider how God dwells in creatures . . . in the plants, giving them life; in the animals, giving them sensation."[86] Recall Fr. Bergoglio telling María Soledad Albisú that even a pigsty was a good place to pray? Now the Ignatian context of that comment falls into place. And, if God dwells in all creation, then, as Ignatius sees it, God "dwells also in myself, giving me existence, life, sensation, and intelligence; and even further, making me his temple, since I am created as a likeness and image of the Divine Majesty. . . ."[87]

That world-engaged attitude is encapsulated in one of the great mantras of Jesuit spirituality: "to find God in all things," a phrase attributed to Ignatius by one of his close companions. The nineteenth-century English Jesuit and poet Gerard Manley Hopkins celebrates the same idea in one of his best-known works: "The world is charged with the grandeur of God."[88] God's presence is everywhere, like a current coursing through everyone and everything. Our human task? To see what is right in front of our eyes, appreciate the world's goodness, and become a loving, just steward of its goods. And, conversely, when the world's human or material goods are being unjustly used or abused, say or do something. As Pope Francis sees it, not all is well in the way we are managing the world's goods: "Today the person counts for nothing, it is coins, it is money that counts. And Jesus, God, gave the world, the whole creation, to the person, to men and women that they might care for it; he did not give it to money."[89]

No wonder that the man who imbibed these ideas as a trainee Jesuit would later urge his seminarians and the rest of us into the midst of this God-charged world. Indeed, he has confessed his worry that "We are losing the attitude of wonder, contemplation, listening to creation; thus we are no longer able to read what Benedict XVI calls 'the rhythm of the love story of God and man.'"[90]

Pope Francis's Jesuit spirituality keeps him connected with reality; God's presence filled those slums through which those Jesuit trainees walked. God was there, and Fr. Bergoglio simply tried to attune them to see that, hear that, even smell that. The same mindset applies to prayer: keep it real, never let it become too remote or abstract. Ignatius reminded Jesuits that they pray to a real person, urging them to talk to Jesus "in the way one friend speaks to another."[91] And Ignatius's spiritual son Francis puts the same idea more picturesquely: "When we talk to God we speak with persons who are concrete and tangible, not some misty, diffused godlike 'god-spray.'"[92]

To summarize this chapter in the Christian terminology of Ignatius and Pope Francis: great leadership is "incarnational"—that is, leaders imitate Jesus, who willingly plunged into a messy world and nonetheless remained undeterred from his vision of how human beings ought to treat one another. Jesus shared the everyday reality of his poorest compatriots, and Jesus presumably did his share of the laundry duty as he and his disciples traveled the road; so today's Christians ought to live and lead in the same style. As Pope Francis put it, "Poverty for us Christians is not a sociological, philosophical or cultural category, no. It is a theological category . . . because our God, the Son of God . . . made Himself poor to walk along the road with us."[93]

If good leadership looks like Jesus in action, what does bad leadership look like? Jesus' foil throughout his worldly sojourn is often the Pharisees, largely because they are hypocrites, who, as Jesus puts it, "tie up heavy burdens, hard to bear, and lay them on shoulders of others; but they themselves are unwilling to lift a finger to move them" (Matthew 23:4).

Or, to put this chapter's theme in secular terms: if you want to lead, get real. Show us that you understand what's really going on in the world. Don't be out of touch; don't hide in an office, behind numbers, or behind ideology. Commit to getting your boots dirty. Inspire us to sacrifice for the team by making sacrifices yourself. Accept accountability for your choices and for their impact on yourself, your family, and the world.

Yes, get real by plunging into the world and getting your feet dirty. But, also, take a step back every day, into a solitary place. The next chapter continues to develop the paradox: great leaders are entirely in the world, but not entirely of it.

6

Kneeling Alone: Withdraw to Find Perspective

Joy is a gift from God. It fills us from within.
—Pope Francis, Homily, May 10, 2013

Fr. Tomás Bradley recalls one of Jorge Mario Bergoglio's priorities: "a daily schedule for prayer, reading, reflection—and a commitment to sustaining it, and being punctual at it." Why? " . . . in order to live with any profundity in life, in order to understand what is happening in one's life, and all the more so when one is going to be exposed to a very active life."

Let's pause for a big yawn. It's no surprise that a priest would intone such pious musings to the baby seminarians. Relevant for them, but hardly riveting fare for the rest of us.

Actually, Fr. Bergoglio's message is even more relevant out here in the world than inside seminary walls. Having lived in both environments, I can attest to that. The stresses outside typically surpass those inside, yet our cupboard of worldly coping skills is pretty barren. This chapter explores that issue while illustrating another transcendent dimension of great leadership. Leaders plunge into the everyday world's challenges and chaos, but they also retreat from the world every day. In this respect, great leadership is as much spiritual as it is world-immersed.

Has Everyone but Me Heard from the Pope?

We start with an anecdote, in fact with a practical tip for readers who read leadership books for concrete takeaways. If your friend is ever elected pope, and you excitedly dash off a "My friend the Pope" message to your e-mail distribution list, delete the pope's address before hitting "Send." Hernán Paredes learned that lesson, one that admittedly may never again come in handy for him or the rest of us (save any cardinals who are curled up with this book).

Paredes, thrilled at his former spiritual director's elevation, quickly e-mailed a few memories and reflections to friends, inadvertently including his friend Jorge Mario Bergoglio's personal e-mail address on the list. Fortunately for Paredes, he had only good things to say.

The point, though, is what happened next: he got a response.

Paredes saved the e-mail (who wouldn't) and proudly displayed it for me on his laptop screen. I'm not quite sure, though, that cyber-memorabilia will get passed down across generations in the way that a proud family might treasure great-grandfather's personally signed letter from Abraham Lincoln. Nor, to be perfectly honest, does Jorge Mario Bergoglio's e-mail font ignite quite the same thrill as ink on paper.

The pope's reply was brief (he had other things on his mind, I'm sure). He thanked Paredes for saying such nice things and requested his prayers.

In fact, Paredes told me that other classmates from seminary days had likewise received personal communications, perhaps no story more poignant than that of Jesuit Fr. Miguel Angel Arias. The previous chapter recounted the pope's Holy Thursday exhortation that priests tend their flock so attentively that they would come to bear the "smell of the sheep."[94] The pope had called Arias in the hours before delivering that very sermon. Despite the crush of appointments that filled the new pope's days, he had not forgotten that his former seminarian lay gravely ill with cancer. He offered his concern and prayers, a leader privately embodying the public message he later delivered in the basilica: stay close to your people and make their needs and struggles your own.

Fr. Arias died that same weekend. Pope Francis celebrated a three-hour Easter Vigil on Saturday night, and on Sunday morning a festive outdoor Mass before tens of thousands, and then delivered the traditional *urbi et orbi* blessing from the central loggia of St. Peter's Basilica. The next morning he delivered another important message, calling Arias's family with his condolences on the day of the funeral.

A handful of others became minor media celebrities after hearing from the pope in less somber circumstances. The switchboard operator at the Jesuit headquarters fielded a direct call when the pope called to speak to the Jesuit General. I happened to be in Rome not long after and dropped in on Rome's newest celebrity, with whom I had chatted in passing once or twice over the years. In a crude mix of Spanish, English, and gesture (I know no Italian), I communicated, "Hey, you're the famous guy who spoke to the pope!" He started recounting the call in animated, rapid-fire Italian, but I was fluent enough in pantomime to catch his drift as he pulled the receiver from his ear, screwed his face into an exasperated scowl, and re-created the eye roll that is universal language for, "Who is this nut on my phone line?—Yeah, right, you're the pope, and I'm the prime minister of Italy." Then he feigns for me the wide-eyed dawning of a realization, "Oh my God—it really is the pope." And he relates how Pope Francis, undoubtedly sensing his rising panic, first asked his name, then sympathetically counseled, "Andrea, *con calma, con calma.*"

A Buenos Aires newspaper-delivery service also received a call, Pope Francis politely informing them what they had surely already concluded: he would be canceling his paper delivery. Thus began the newspaperman's fifteen minutes of fame, during which he volunteered a telling detail that enhanced the pope's credibility as an advocate for environmental stewardship. The pope would visit the news kiosk at the end of each month and hand over a pile of thirty (or thirty one, or twenty-eight) rubber bands, the rubber bands that had wrapped his paper each morning.[95]

Jesuit brother Mario Rafael Rausch got a call, as usual, on his March 23 birthday, and the priest who served as Cardinal Bergoglio's personal secretary confirmed that every priest in Buenos Aires had a direct line on which he could call the cardinal.[96]

Gee, am I the only one who hasn't heard from the pope and doesn't know how to track him down?

These charming vignettes affirm last chapter's themes: stay in touch, remain grounded, treat each person as a uniquely dignified individual, not as a mere functionary or some interchangeable box on an organization chart.

Delegation, Wisely Applied

But here's Pope Francis's new reality: however he managed, as Cardinal Bergoglio, to sustain this "high touch" routine up to now, the papal workload won't allow him to place every phone call, man an open phone line for the world's 400,000 or so Catholic priests, and manage a newspaper subscription, much less handle every piece of paperwork that finds its way into the Vatican. In fact, in the run-up to this papal election, cardinals had already been thumping their desks (OK, I guess cardinals are too dignified to thump their desks). Cardinals had averred in discreet Christian charity that the Vatican is a bureaucratic black hole: issues and paperwork flow in, resurfacing eons later.

Many new leaders are quickly swamped by the volume and complexity of issues that assault them. How does a new pope—or a hospital manager or a parent for that matter—possibly keep up with it all?

The counterintuitive, even paradoxical answer? Step back from it all. Remember the counsel that Fr. Bradley recalls from Fr. Bergoglio: if your life will be highly active, you need to commit to a regimen of reflection in order to survive.

The pace, volume, complexity, and volatility endemic to today's working life all conspire to raise stress unmanageably, mire us in overwork, erode our decision-making skills, distract our focus, and, as a result, threaten our very well-being. The National Institute for Occupational Safety and Health has estimated that 40 percent of all workers feel overworked and stressed to the point of anxiety or depression.[97]

We all know these symptoms, but leadership experts and organizational-behavior consultants proffer not cures but Band-Aids, like better time management and vigorous delegation, which address the problem's practical aspects but leave untreated its transcendent dimensions, the imperative for introspective reflection. We have believed for too long that reflection is "too soft" or that it is "outside the proper scope of a workplace" to discuss how executives might keep themselves recollected through reflection or even, God forbid, private prayer. So after beginning with a discussion of the practical (delegation), we'll push beyond the comfort zone to consider the transcendent (recollection and prayer).

It is common knowledge by now that lousy leaders micromanage and good leaders delegate. We're better motivated and more productive when we can exercise some control over our work: give me a realistic goal and the resources to achieve it, but trust me to figure out how to accomplish it. Good parents learn that increasing their children's responsibilities, along with their freedoms, teaches them how to cope, solve problems, and own their lives, more so than they learn from constant supervision and overcorrection. Common sense tells us that no executive will understand every legal issue better than a competent legal counsel, or every manufacturing question better than the production pro, and so on. Finally, there's even a spiritual dimension to delegation: if you respect me as gifted, even made in God's image, how could you not dedicate yourself to coaching, training, browbeating, encouraging, or cajoling me into flourishing to the best of my God-given talents, including learning to handle challenges through my own initiative?

Recall Ethan Berman, the earlier profiled one-time chief executive of a financial services firm, who took the spectacularly counterintuitive step of urging his board of directors to pay him less than they had planned? His experience there offers some insight into delegation and trust.

He oversaw his firm's rapid growth from about twenty-five employees to more than a thousand. In the early days, Ethan says, "I would run into someone in the hallway, and we might end up making a strategic decision right there." A business school professor approvingly labeled the early company an "ad-hocracy" rather than a "bureaucracy." That is, while gargantuan companies lumber along bureaucratically, nimbler "ad-hocracies" can outmaneuver them by brisk decision making (even in hallways). But rapid growth presents challenges. As Ethan put it, "once you have hundreds of people, some of them in Tokyo, they don't get to chime in on the conversations in the New York hallway, so you need to add another whole layer to the decision-making process."

The trick is adding bureaucracy without becoming bureaucratic, which is where delegation can help. Ethan faced a challenge that confronts every individual promoted to manage a small team, every small team manager promoted to lead layers of middle managers, or every Argentine cardinal elevated to pastor the universal Church. After Ethan hired the company's first sales manager, a field about which Ethan professes zero knowledge, he nonetheless couldn't help second-guessing the new manager's plans. After all, he had become used to participating in every decision; it can be hard to relinquish that hands-on instinct, especially when conscientious micromanagement of detail was what speeded one's advancement through the organization's ranks in the first place. But after weeks of meddling in the new hire's plans, Ethan had an epiphany. "Hey, if I made a mistake hiring this guy, I ought to let him go. But if I hired the right guy, I need to trust him to do his job." He backed off and let the guy run his department, very successfully as it turned out.

The Balance of Authority and Trust

With growth and complexity, delegation becomes imperative. And with delegation, trust becomes imperative. Ignatius of Loyola's "start-up" presents another worthwhile case study: within a generation of its launch, the Jesuits had grown from ten personal friends to a 5,000-strong multinational religious order functioning on four continents. And though Ignatius worked in the sleepy sixteenth century, before Harvard Business School had opened its doors, he intuitively "got" the concept of delegation.

Surprisingly, perhaps. After all, one typically associates religious orders with vows of poverty, chastity, and obedience, and Ignatius famously championed the latter. In one memorable if unflattering image, Ignatius said that a Jesuit under obedience should be like "an old man's staff which serves in any place and in any manner whatsoever in which the holder wishes to use it."[98] How's that for motivating imagery?

But optimal results follow when the willingness to flex authority is married to equally aggressive delegation; plenty are the managers who habitually lean too heavily one way or the other, but rare are those who do both well. For example, Ignatius could dispatch his best friend, Francis Xavier, to Asia on a couple of days' notice for what, in the sixteenth century, was almost certainly a one-way trip, given the long, slow sea voyage. Yet after mandating him to pursue this strategic geographic priority for the fledgling Jesuits, Ignatius relied completely on Francis Xavier's judgment to organize virtually every aspect of

Jesuit operations there—a strong exercise of authority coupled with equally bold delegation.

In fact, despite Ignatius's insistence that obedient Jesuits be like "old men's staffs," his letters to subordinates are heavily sprinkled with sentences such as "I leave everything to your judgment and I will consider best whatever you shall decide" or "Whatever means you shall judge to be better in our Lord, I fully approve . . . you are in closer touch with affairs where you are" or "Oliver, cut your suit according to your cloth; only let us know how you have acted."[99]

Leader to the Change Resistant

Will Pope Francis show the same mastery of delegation as did his spiritual father Ignatius? One early incident seems telling. The cardinal-overseer of a key Vatican department, needing to fill the slot of a second-in-charge, recounted in an interview that the pope had asked him, "Who do you want as your secretary [i.e., your number two]? Give me three names." "So I gave him three names," the cardinal recounted. "But [the pope] said, 'Of the three, which is the one you want?' I said this one, Carballo. [The pope] said, 'Good, fine.' And he gave us José Carballo [José Rodríguez Carballo, OFM]."

The cardinal's next comment aptly summarizes our discussion of trust and delegation: "It's a wonderful, simple way of doing things: I trust you, I trust Carballo, so that's it . . . He [the pope] doesn't complicate it."[100]

Actually, on second thought, that doesn't quite sum up the discussion at all: it's way more complicated than that. The pope faces a classically difficult organizational problem. He was elected, in part, as a change agent. No change agent succeeds alone. He needs a coalition of like-minded lieutenants to help drive the culture change he envisions, but, presumably, some of the lieutenants are part of the problem. If he doesn't delegate aggressively to his team, he fails. But what if the team is change-resistant? If the leader delegates to hidebound bureaucrats who don't share his vision, he also loses: nothing grounds new initiatives to a halt like the determined non-determination of powerful bureaucrats.

Vatican watchers have noted that Pope Francis has taken an unprecedentedly long time to confirm in office the incumbent Vatican department heads ("dicastery" heads in Vatican-speak) that he inherited. Why the delay? He knows these are crucially important decisions for the future of the Church and, I suspect, is assessing which of the team are willing to help lead the Church where the pope wants to take it.

As he weighs those important decisions, I am sure he is exercising a profound yet widely neglected tool that is even more essential as leaders cope with complexity and change: the ability to withdraw for quiet reflection.

Not Boot Camp but Quiet Reflection

Once we managers delegate, what do we invariably do with the time that we have freed up? We fill it up immediately with more activity and more work. In the process, we slowly erode our ability to focus, and, what's more, slowly drive ourselves and everyone around us nuts.

As we entered the new millennium, a steady trickle of articles in the *Harvard Business Review* (HBR) started focusing on two related problems: obsessive busyness and the inability to step back and reflect. A 2002 article from two European business school professors noted that executives will "tell you that the resource they lack most is time . . . But if you watch them, here's what you'll see: They rush from meeting to meeting, check their e-mail constantly, extinguish fire after fire, and make countless phone calls. In short, you'll see an astonishing amount of fast-moving activity that allows almost no time for reflection." The authors called this chaotic, not particularly purposeful fire-fighting "unproductive busyness" and "active nonaction."[101]

A year later, Henry Mintzberg, a dean of modern leadership thinking, took up the same theme in a cowritten article: "Managers who are sent off to development courses these days often find themselves being welcomed to 'boot camp.' . . . But this is wrongheaded . . . Most managers we know already live boot camp every day . . . These days, what managers desperately need is to stop and think, to step back and reflect thoughtfully on their experiences."[102]

But while consensus seems to be emerging that we have an epidemic of unproductive busyness, prescriptions for healing it are few and often derided by the macho business world. One HBR interview offered an unintentionally humorous case in point. A mind-body researcher ventured that small-group corporate brainstorming sessions might improve if preceded by mind-clearing "relaxation response" exercises. "I ask [the executives] to close their eyes. . . . Every time they breathe out, they should silently say a word or phrase that is personally meaningful to them, like 'calm' or 'peace.' If they happen to be religious, they might say something like the first line of the twenty-third psalm. . . ."[103]

The very next words from the apparently astonished interviewer's mouth sum up the dilemma: "It's hard to imagine any leader doing that. It sounds much too soft." End of discussion.

We all know there is a problem: the "active nonaction," the endless maelstrom of texts and calls, the work-well temporarily emptied through delegation but immediately refilled with more stuff, the inability to devote twenty undivided minutes to a colleague's presentation without sneaking under-the-table glances at the smartphone (by the way, we notice), the smartphone that must be turned on just as the airplane wheels are hitting the tarmac (and curse the phone company for wasting fifteen of my valuable seconds while I have to wait for these stupid messages to download). Everyone knows we need to claw out from under the faux urgency and step off the unproductive treadmill. But how? Well, Pope Francis, true to his Ignatian tradition, might have a suggestion about what to do:

Nothing.

Or, what may look like nothing to superficial observers is, to Pope Francis, the most consequential thing he does every day. Make that multiple times every day.

A Pope in Solitary Silence

A new chief executive ought to launch his first day in office with the most valuable tasks he can conceive, like a meeting with key lieutenants, briefings on strategy or finances, or sending a company-wide memo to underscore key priorities. Pope Francis likewise put first things first on day one by doing the most important thing he could conceive: a private visit to pray at St. Mary Major Basilica, including at the altar where Jesuit founder Ignatius of Loyola had centuries earlier celebrated his first Mass as a priest.

The image of the pope in solitary silence on day one of his administration as the minutes ticked by—he didn't look like a guy rushing through a photo op—ought to become an iconic leadership image, like that of the empty papal limousine or the foot-washing of juvenile delinquents. But it won't become iconic simply because nothing seemed to be happening: no discussions, travel, meetings, or computers crunching numbers in the background—in short, nothing that would fit our stereotypes of worthwhile activity. The leader's quiet moments are instead considered "downtime" at best and wasted time at worst.

But in the course of those prayerful minutes, Pope Francis was doing some of the most valuable things any leader can do. He was praying, of course, but in the very act of praying he was recalling his sense of mission and the values he needs to model, decluttering his mind to refocus on priorities, breaking from sheer busyness in order to reenergize himself, and regaining perspective by acknowledging that the world is not ultimately under his control anyway.

In fact, that 8:30 a.m. basilica visit was almost certainly not his first reflective moment that day. Years earlier, two journalists had asked what personal possessions he would save in the event of fire, and Fr. Bergoglio named his appointment book and his breviary—"I'm very attached to the breviary," he said.[104] The breviary (the Latin word connotes "brief" or "short"), used daily by all Catholic priests, is comprised of prayers, biblical readings, and other spiritual writings. Between the pages of his own years-old, well-worn copy, the pope has tucked other mementos over the years: some of his grandmother's letters and a favorite poem.

More important for us, though, is how a priest uses the breviary, dipping into it for short reflective periods at various points each day. Pope Francis told the journalists that it is "the first thing I open in the morning and the last thing I close before going to bed."[105] Presumably, he consulted that breviary before beginning that first papal day and spent his last waking moments with it that same night. Well, perhaps not always "waking" moments. He confessed to one group of visitors that, during late-night prayer sessions, "Sometimes I doze off, the fatigue of the day makes you fall asleep, but God understands."[106]

Chances are, the pope had other moments of private reflection that day (and every day), judging by the regimen he suggested to—imposed upon—Paredes,

Gauffin, Bradley, and the seminarians of their era. Each day at noon and at 5:00 p.m., a bell summoned the seminarians. Some ran to the chapel from studies, the community farm, or domestic labors; still others paused in their classrooms or dormitory. And then? A puzzled outside observer would tell us that these dozens of young men had all hurried together in order to do, well, nothing. Some knelt and others sat, all wordlessly. They would silently pass about a quarter hour together, neither singing hymns, chanting prayers, nor listening to a sermon from Fr. Bergoglio; in fact, he joined them in silence.

Recollection for Those on the Move

I know what they were doing because I had often done it myself. Jesuits, in their strange predilection for arcane Latin terminology, still refer to this discipline as the *examen* (the Latin root word suggests a process of "examining" or "testing" oneself), what a modern person might call a mental pit stop. Along with the Spiritual Exercises, it is one of the most distinctive disciplines of Jesuit spirituality. During those precious few undistracted minutes—undistracted, i.e., no Facebooking or texting, please—one accomplishes at least three life-giving tasks. First, remind yourself why you are grateful as a human being. Second, lift your horizon for a moment by calling to mind your ultimate sense of purpose and values or some habitual failing you hope to address. And third, mentally review the past few hours to extract some insight that might help in the next few hours. If you were irritable with colleagues or patients, what might have been happening? Those within a religious tradition, like Jesuits, reflect on how God was present to them in the encounters of the day thus far, make amends for their shortcomings, and ask God's blessings for the next few hours.

The genius of this simple process becomes compelling when we consider the external environments that we managers, or popes, or parents must navigate each day: we surf a tide of e-mails, texts, meetings, calls, day-to-day problems, and distractions. We never find time to step back. The fallout is obvious: I'm stressed about the car malfunction that had me at the repair shop half the day and end up lashing out at my teenager, who had nothing to do with it. I finish the workday without attacking my number-one priority because I was swept along by lesser day-to-day concerns. I never focus my best thinking in a concentrated fashion on any one issue because three or four issues are always rambling around my head; or, I slowly drift into an ethical mess of a transaction because I never stopped along the way to ask myself, "Hang on, is this the kind of thing we really should be doing?"

The practice, seemingly tailor-made to suit today's chaotic lifestyles, was in fact Ignatius of Loyola's ingenious solution to a dilemma presented by his highly activist vision for Jesuit life. As we've seen, Ignatius envisioned his Jesuits fully immersed in the world as teachers, pastoral counselors, or missionaries in far-flung lands—to use Fr. Bergoglio's imagery, getting their feet so dirty in the world's barrios that they carried the smell of the sheep. That activist lifestyle was incompatible with scurrying back to chapel every few hours for communal prayer—that is, the periodic chanting of the Divine Office, the hallmark of monastic-style religious orders. So the examen, undertaken individually, whenever and wherever circumstances permitted, would keep Jesuits recollected and God-focused, despite their activist lifestyles.

So why did Fr. Bergoglio make all those seminarians do it together? His approach initially had me stumped. Why summon us together for a personal stock-taking that each Jesuit must, by definition, perform privately? And why overlay a fixed schedule, complete with bell ringing, on a discipline that Ignatius had designed to assure maximum scheduling flexibility? It all sounded a little musty and old-fashioned to me, the way Jesuits had done things a century earlier, long abandoned by the time I went through training. Yes, I had been expected to do my examens daily, but even as a novice, I decided when and where to do them; we punched no time clock at the chapel door, and no clipboard-wielding quality-control cleric trailed us. I suspect I would have chafed under Fr. Bergoglio's more regimented approach (and, in fact, at least some of his Jesuit contemporaries apparently did question it).

But after working on Wall Street and stumbling across a saying of one wise Francis, I think I can perceive what the other wise Francis was up to. The one Francis is early-seventeenth-century French bishop Francis de Sales. When asked how much daily prayer was necessary, he is reported to have counseled that a half hour is sufficient each day, except when one is too busy.

In that case, pray twice as long, an hour.

Ignore the time frames (and the religiosity if you are not religious), but focus on the core insight: the busier you are, the more essential it is to remain recollected. And I suspect that the second Francis, the current pope, may have had something like that in mind when devising his seminarians' prayer schedule. As for me, I needed the worldly investment-banking environment, not placid seminary precincts, to get that point.

When I was a Jesuit novice, I did my daily examen unfailingly, no bell ringing or regimented schedule needed. For one thing, I was the Jesuit version of a Boy Scout: I always did the right thing. But for another, take my word for it: life moves pretty slowly in a novitiate; not much happens anyway. It was not like I was tearing myself away from rock concerts or whitewater rafting runs for each fifteen-minute prayer break.

And if action was scarce in the seminary, so was temptation. The environment was unrelievedly (even oppressively) spiritual. It was easy to sustain the discipline because the environment was sleepy and serene, but, ironically, for those very same reasons, I really didn't need the discipline: I was focused and recollected, anyway, because the novitiate presented few distractions.

Then I advanced to the next phase of Jesuit life, at one point simultaneously completing two degrees while also teaching catechism, doing community chores, and juggling other obligations. In fact, I was so busy with my many worthy pursuits that I couldn't even squeeze in a ten-minute reflective examen on some days . . . and then I couldn't squeeze it in on many days. I was dutifully playing my part as a seminarian, but losing the plot—who am I, and why am I doing these activities?

How Not to Spin

I wasn't really enlightened about the value of these mental pit stops until well into investment-banker life, when grinding through oppressively full schedules made even the busiest seminary day seem leisurely. One afternoon, fed up with battling an endless inflowing tide of messages that no amount of work could make recede, I retreated. I strolled from my Tokyo office to the greenbelt surrounding the Imperial Palace. Oddly, I got no less done by the end of that day, despite the time I had "wasted," because I had come back more focused.

So I started a habit of purposefully wasting a few minutes each day, later on in London strolling from my Victoria Embankment office up to St. Bride's Church for a daily mental pit stop.

A light bulb went off one afternoon when I asked a coworker how a talented recent hire of hers was adjusting to the company. She shook her head and chuckled and said, "He's spinning," the latest victim of a familiar occupational hazard. This capable employee, battered by the sheer torrent of work, didn't know where to turn first and consequently spun one way and then another in a confused frenzy of busyness, doing much, accomplishing little, and lacking focus.

"That guy . . ." I could almost see the words floating out of my mouth but grabbed them back before uttering a sentence that would have been incomprehensible to my colleague: "That guy needs to start doing his examen."

I almost laughed out loud. I didn't know where the thought had come from and probably hadn't thought about the discipline for years. Until that moment, it hadn't dawned on me that I had been doing my own version of an examen during those Tokyo or London lunchtime strolls, not in the formal sense that Ignatius (or Fr. Bergoglio) might recommend, but purposefully enough to keep me focused and recollected. My investment-banking experience had validated Francis de Sales's witty observation: precisely when my corporate life was busiest did I really, really need to allow time for reflection, far more so than during the relatively sleepy novitiate days.

But you have to commit to it. If it is not a habit, it doesn't happen because other more pressing (if ultimately less important) tasks will always crowd recollection from the schedule. Ten minutes of personal peace can always wait; finishing the memo always seems like it can't. Customers (or students, or patients) always keep calling, but Fr. Bergoglio doesn't call to remind us to recollect ourselves. And so we turn ourselves into hamsters on hamster wheels: spinning, but not necessarily moving forward.

So I started looking at Fr. Bergoglio's bells and the herding of those seminarians into chapel not from the perspective of a former seminarian, but from that of a former banker. And I kept thinking of Fr. Bradley's recollection that Fr. Bergoglio had stressed "a daily schedule for prayer, reading, reflection—and a commitment to sustaining it, and being punctual at it . . . in order to understand what is happening in one's life, and all the more so when one is going to be exposed to a very active life."

Contemplative Even in Action

Fr. Bergoglio understood that life's pace is so intense, the bleat of media so omnipresent, the demands of "feet dirty" leadership so unrelenting, that spinning invariably befalls those who don't build sacred space into their schedules. He was trying to drill a discipline so deeply into his seminarians that the routine would survive once they progressed from seminary and had to start taking full accountability for managing their own daily schedules.

Fr. Bergoglio was well aligned with his spiritual mentor, Ignatius of Loyola, who likewise envisioned Jesuits fully "in" the world, but not completely "of" it. For fully in the world, Ignatius used the image that fully formed Jesuits would have the disposition and skills to "run in the path of Christ our Lord."[107] Run, he said, not walk. He exhorted them to live "with one foot raised," ever ready to seize the next opportunity. He structured the Jesuit order to accommodate this action-oriented vision, unshackling Jesuits from many of the constraining conventions of late medieval religious orders, including, controversially at the time, from the obligation to engage in communal prayer multiple times each day.

But Ignatius likewise perceived that a Jesuit living "with one foot raised" would quickly become rootless without a well-disciplined interior life. And running can easily deteriorate into spinning—the former is purposeful, the latter frenetic and unfocused.

That's why, while the activist mindset was essential to his organizational vision, equally essential and absolutely nonnegotiable was the discipline of personal prayer and recollection, above all the mental pit stops he called the examen.

When it works, action and reflection reinforce each other symbiotically as part of a virtuous circle. In fact, when it works best, it's hard to draw sharp distinctions between prayer and work. Look, for example, at a striking (and challenging) assertion of Cardinal Bergoglio's some years ago, as part of dialogues with Rabbi Abraham Skorka, a friend of Cardinal Bergoglio's and a leading rabbi in Argentina, that were published as *Sobre el cielo y la tierra* ("On Heaven and Earth").[108] This chapter and the previous one have dealt with the dynamic relation between world and spirit, reflection and action. Cardinal Bergoglio pushed that dynamic relation even further, asserting that righteous action is prayer; and, conversely, prayer without worldly follow-up is not prayer but hypocrisy:

> The act of justice that concretizes itself in help of one's neighbor is prayer. If not, one falls into the sin of hypocrisy, which is like a schizophrenia of the soul . . . the Lord is my brother and my brother is hungry. If a person does not take care of his brother, he is not able to talk with the Father about his brother, with God.[109]

With that discipline of action reinforced by reflection all day long, punctuated by solitary, prayerful breaks, one becomes, to use an image coined by one of Ignatius of Loyola's closest lieutenants, *simul in actione contemplativus*, contemplatives even in action.

But without that discipline, nonstop busyness may become nothing more than "a tale told by an idiot, full of sound and fury, signifying nothing," to paraphrase Shakespeare, in *Macbeth*.

Not Just for Leaders

The same is true for the rest of us, whatever our religious or spiritual beliefs. Contemporary life—as parents, executives, teachers, whatever—has become too frenetically busy for us to allow ourselves to become frenetically busy spinners who never lift our heads high enough to see where we are going.

We need to carve out time every day for personal reflection, and, unfortunately, "carve out" is the right phrase. It will not happen without a commitment. The time will not simply present itself. No manager will demand that we put down the phone, shut off the computer, and just reflect. And we can't rely on a Fr. Bergoglio to summon us for twice-daily reflections with a bell: he's busy now himself, and, besides, with Vatican functionaries pulling him this way and that all day, he needs to be vigilant to carve out his own time for reflection. Fortunately, we don't have to rely on him or his bell because even the dumbest of smartphone alarms can be programmed to chime us into a few moments of nonaction each day—call it the "Bergoglio app," or the "*simul in actione contemplativus* app."

To be sure, Pope Francis would chase me around Vatican Square with a stick if I suggested that his examen, the prayerful moments he spends with his breviary, the Mass he attends, or the Rosary he prays daily were completely equivalent to a manager's meditative five minutes in a closed office. He is praying. He believes—and I with him—that an intimate one-on-one communion with life's author is occurring, even when it hardly feels like it, even when, as the pope has confessed, one drifts off to sleep in its midst.

But even if prayer's purpose is other-worldly, it nonetheless brings worldly benefits. And even if what happens during prayer is mysterious, those worldly benefits are obvious. And one does not have to share Pope Francis's religious beliefs or prayer traditions to reap the human rewards that accrue from recollected silence each day.

After all, imagine the pope in his private chapel near midnight, those Argentine seminarians hurrying together after studies or manual labor, the Muslim answering the call to prayer, or the executive who closes her office door for a few peaceful minutes. To be sure, something unique is happening in each of these cases; each is in many ways unlike the others. But in other important respects, all these cases are alike. The very same things may be happening, namely:

- We express the gratitude that is core to every great humanistic or spiritual tradition, and consequently enjoy the peace and happiness that flow from the simple act of expressing thanks.
- We lift our horizons above the quotidian affairs that bombard and distract us; we recall that we are here for some larger purpose and have committed to stand for certain values.
- We take stock of the hours just passed, the people, problems, and opportunities that came our way, the joys and sufferings we saw, and we reflect on these in the light of our human or spiritual beliefs. We make amends, according to our tradition, for the moments when we haven't been our best selves.

And then it's time to put the past behind us and resume "living with one foot raised," seizing anew the only moment we know we've been given to live: this moment right now. The following chapter takes up the theme of living in the present moment.

7

Build on Stones: Live in the Present and Reverence Tradition

Fidelity is always a change, a blossoming, a growth.
—Pope Francis, Interview, November 2007

This chapter title may sound like feel-good gibberish to those who prefer a more straightforward "kick ass and take names" style leadership; and the next chapter, all about "creating the future," may seem like mere sloganeering.

Well, if "create the future" seems too vague, please meditate on the alphabet: *B* is for all those Blockbuster videocassette rental stores you no longer see in your neighborhood; *K* is for the Kodak film you no longer buy; and *X* is for the Xerox machine you needed to make copies before all files became digital. *A* is for anyone still clueless enough to imagine that the tumult of change that has upturned every other walk of life will bypass theirs.

If it's impossible to picture what "reverencing tradition" might entail, visit a few white-collar criminals serving jail terms because they didn't consider integrity, justice, or respect for others to be enduring values worth standing for.

And "live in the present"? Heck, just walk around your workplace and start counting the colleagues who don't appreciate the impact they could make at this very moment if they weren't stewing over an organizational decision or office snub from one week (or one year) ago, then add the many other colleagues who focus less on the opportunity right in front of them than the one they wish they had.

Balancing this leadership triptych of past, present, and future is difficult in any business, but incredibly so in Pope Francis's "business." I have been lucky

89

enough to work with and for organizations that honored their stated core values. But at the end of the day, we knew those values statements had been crafted by folks like us with flip charts in conference rooms; when those statements no longer served us, we changed them. And the penalties for violating them? Well, it depended. If you were a "rainmaker" who regularly showered the organization with downpours of lucrative new business deals, maybe we ignored your disrespectful treatment of colleagues—as long as you kept making rain, you got a hall pass from core values class.

The Pope's Challenge

It's different with the pope's "business," as with any revealed religion. Some of the values, convictions, and practices are considered not merely enduring but eternal. Sacred biblical texts, adherents believe, are not simply dashed off by imaginative story writers but in some mysterious way reflect revealed, immutable truths.

Thus Pope Francis's daunting leadership challenge. The Catholic Church is buffeted by the same intense change that assaults Blockbuster, Kodak, and the rest of us. The Church must adapt; that is not an opinion but a plain fact whenever human organizations confront profound environmental change. Indeed, for decades now, popes have echoed a mantra of "new ardor, methods, and expressions."[110]

Few would rate the revitalization and renewal effort a rousing success. Many Catholics would argue that their Church has changed far too little, others that it has changed far too much or in the wrong ways, and still others would condemn those impertinent enough to dare rate their Church's success at all.

Welcome to Pope Francis's world, and, to an extent, the leader's world in every profession. "Uneasy lies the head that wears a crown," as Shakespeare put it in *Henry IV*, and that is above all true as leaders balance past tradition, present realities, and future possibilities. This chapter and the next focus on one of the most difficult balancing acts any leader confronts: how to live in the present, show proper respect for one's values and tradition, and drive an organization into the future. We'll see how the pope's Jesuit tradition might help him and us do that well.

Live in the Present: Seize This Moment

I once heard a deeply affecting radio interview with a gentleman who had played on Manchester United's extraordinarily talented soccer team that contended for the 1958 European Cup championship. After a drawn match in then-Yugoslavia catapulted Man United into the semifinal round of play, the exhausted but happy team began traveling home, a long journey that included a pre-jet age refueling stop in Munich.

The weather was terrible. The players sat on a runway and watched snow falling. A layer of slush coated the airfield by the time the plane had refueled. The pilots began accelerating down the runway for takeoff but aborted their run and repositioned themselves for a second attempt. The weather deteriorated as they revved the engines and tried again, and the once-festive players surely turned tense as the plane throttled forward. And then slowed: another effort abandoned.

The third effort was more determined, too determined. The plane skidded off the runway, crashed through a fence, clipped a house, smashed into a tree, and a burst fuel tank ignited a fire. Nearly half of the forty-four passengers perished, including eight young Manchester United footballers and three team staff. The death of the young footballers came little more than a decade after some 400,000 young British soldiers had perished in World War II: a devastated Britain anguished anew to see their youth once again cut down in life's prime.

Decades later, a surviving player recalled the day's events and the death of his teammate friends during this radio interview and concluded, as best I recall, with words like these: "And, you know, from that day until now, I've never done anything I didn't want to do." The moment had become an inflection point, a hinge in his life history.

I might have expressed the sentiment differently, but I understood the point. Life is short. Don't fritter it away on what's not important to you. Don't do what you might regret later. And, conversely, seize each day's precious opportunity; one like it may or may not come your way again. A one-time investment-banking colleague of mine had coached track and field before entering the finance business; before almost every race, he told me, he would lean in close to a racer's face, hold his or her gaze, and simply say, "Run like this is the last race you'll ever run in your life."

None of these ideas were new to me. Both Jorge Mario Bergoglio and I had heard similar refrains during our Jesuit formation, when novice directors would counsel: *Age quod agis*, "Do what you are doing." (A companion idea had fallen out of use by my era, likely in deference to my Latin-challenged generation: *qui fecit nimis, fecit nihil*, loosely put, "the one who tries to do too much ends up accomplishing nothing.")

Granted, *age quod agis* doesn't quite inspire like "Run like it may be the last race of your life" or that Man United player's conclusion after watching teammates die. Truth be told, we've all heard sayings such as "seize the day" so often that they have ceased to wield much impact.

But their truth remains. I hired lots of talented young people over time, many in a hurry up the corporate ladder, but not all understood that the surest way to each new rung was superb execution of the task in front of them. I also serve as chair of a large hospital system that envisions "improving the health of the people and communities we serve." The only way to that vision is relentless attention to quality and safety during the millions of interventions that unfold in hospitals each day, from administering medications to helping patients transfer from beds into wheelchairs to performing microscopically precise neurosurgeries.

But we are digging deeper than maxims, trying to unearth the building blocks of a leadership spirituality, a set of commitments solid enough to sustain and drive a meaningful life. And, the above ideas seem to figure powerfully among Pope Francis's convictions. Indeed, he worked hard to drill them into the Jesuit seminarians he coached. Fr. Tomás Bradley ticked off for me some half-dozen themes that Fr. Bergoglio used to stress, including this one: "Dedicate yourself to what you're doing and do it well." That was Fr. Bergoglio's take on *age quod agis*.

Bradley remembers the seminary rector emphasizing "excellence in their studies," and "demanding hours of daily study, and many times saying to us, 'we run the risk of scattering ourselves in too many directions.'" Fr. James Kelly, an Irish Jesuit who taught at the seminary in those days, told me he was sometimes surprised that Bergoglio was as well liked as he was by many of the seminarians. Why? I asked. "Well," Kelly told me, "he was most, most demanding. He pushed them very hard at their studies." Perhaps, like those athletes trained to run as if each race was the last of their lives, the students appreciated the disciplined focus on the task at hand that was being bred into them.

Fr. Bergoglio "walked that talk" of seizing the present moment. In the series of interviews later published as *El Jesuita*, then-Cardinal Bergoglio recalled an afternoon when he had committed to conduct a retreat at a convent outside Buenos Aires.[111] Though running a bit late for his train, he nonetheless squeezed in a few moments of prayer at the Buenos Aires cathedral. As he rose to leave, a young man who seemed disoriented by medication or alcohol approached to ask then-Bishop Bergoglio to hear his confession. Now badly pressed for time, he begged off; assuring the man that a priest would arrive soon to hear confessions, he excused himself and hurried off.

"But after walking a little ways," the cardinal recalled, "I felt a tremendous shame. I returned and told him, 'the father is going to be late. I will hear your confession.'"[112] Afterward, he tarried still longer, accompanying the young man to a side altar where they prayed side by side for the young man's well-being. Finally, Bergoglio left for the train station, no doubt rehearsing the apology he would offer the nuns for arriving late and disrupting their schedule.

Except he didn't miss his train. It, too, was delayed, delayed in fact until just a moment or so after he hopped on board, as if God had held the train just long enough for him to have heard that confession and still reach the convent on time. Neither I nor Bishop Bergoglio, I'm sure, imagined that God literally inconvenienced hundreds of other commuters so that the priest could catch a train.

But the whole experience deeply unsettled him. As soon as he got back to Buenos Aires, he immediately went to his own confessor. "If you do not hear my confession, I will not be able to celebrate Mass tomorrow," he said, because the incident weighed so heavily on his conscience. "I was playing Tarzan," he recounted, absorbed in efficiently dispatching paperwork, preaching Masses, giving retreats, and juggling the other duties of an important bishop. "Somehow I was saying, 'Look how good I am, what great things I am able to do,' my attitude was all about pride."[113] In a sense, he was so blinded by self-importance and his impressive to-do list that he could not recognize the needy young man right in front of him.

Journalists have plucked various stories from the interviews that form *El Jesuita*, but I've yet to see that one highlighted: in a journalist's view, nothing important seems to have happened. Yet it crystallizes a life skill that every busy leader knows is important: when and how to dedicate yourself completely to the opportunity in front of you.

Call it the "mysticism of the present moment," or, for the nonreligious, the "you-just-never-know effect." An acquaintance of mine retired after serving as managing partner of one of the world's top accounting firms. A few years later, he was walking down a Manhattan street when a thirtysomething guy in a suit veered up to him. "Ken! I'm so happy to run into you! Not a month goes by when I don't think of that meeting we had with Such-and-such company, how you handled them when they wanted us to pursue that accounting treatment you didn't feel comfortable with, and what you told me afterwards about integrity. You know, that really shaped who I am today, and I always felt bad that I never had the chance to thank you personally . . . so now I can."

Ken chuckled before telling me, "You know something, Chris? I didn't remember that guy, and I didn't remember that client meeting he was referring to!"

You just never know. You never know when "just doing my job" or a casual conversation with a friend may become a pivotal moment in someone else's life. How many parents have discovered that the most important discussions with their kids are often unanticipated, occurring, for example, during a routine commute to school: if they hadn't been attentive at that moment, waiting for the traffic light to change, some crucial bit of conversation might not have happened. And, in the case of this busy bishop, it became clear that it was more important to hear a disturbed young man's confession than to rush off to tackle the next thing on the to-do list. Ultimately, the only opportunity you know you have is the one that sits before you right now. What might be routine and forgettable to you may be vital to someone else.

Another story of Fr. Bergoglio in the confessional further illustrates the point. In *El Jesuita*, Bergoglio revealed that he always asks a young parent who visits him for confession: "Do you play with your children?"[114]

Do you play with your children!? I was moved to read that simple yet profound question. Many of us pursue demanding, remunerative jobs because we want to provide the best for the children we love; yet, in perverse consequence, we don't get to see them enough or are too distracted and exhausted to be fully present to them, to listen to their ramblings about what happened in second grade today, to play the same silly game for the hundredth time, or to devote ourselves to the thousands more interactions that epitomize the mysticism of the present moment.

Fr. Bergoglio seems to have lived in the present both in day-to-day affairs (hearing that disturbed man's confession) but also as a more encompassing philosophy. He joined the Jesuits in part to become a missionary and go to Japan. Not allowed to do so because of concerns that his earlier respiratory illness had weakened his constitution, he faced a fundamental choice: to stew forever over the chance denied him or to seize each new role laid before him from then on.

That included, ironically, the role of not being pope. When, by most accounts, he finished a clear second in the 2005 papal balloting, any of us could have told him what to do: prepare for the next time around. Widen your support base among the cardinals, land an influential post in Rome, and cultivate "thought leaders" who are good at discreetly promoting ambitious people who need to camouflage their unseemly ambitions.

Instead, after the conclave that elected Pope Benedict, Cardinal Bergoglio hurried back to Buenos Aires, almost as far as one could get from Rome. He gave few interviews. He allocated a disproportionate share of his time to the poor, who, you may have noticed, don't get to vote for pope. Instead of looking ahead, he looked at the tasks right in front of him, embodying the advice of Ecclesiastes: "Whatever your hand finds to do, do it with all your might" (Ecclesiastes 9:10).

For Fr. Bergoglio's final Jesuit posting before he was named a bishop, he was assigned to work as a spiritual guide and house confessor for Jesuits in Córdoba. Even self-described Catholic commentators have since interpreted the assignment through the lens of backroom politics and intrigue: Fr. Bergoglio wasn't given a big management job, which must indicate that his Jesuit confreres had exiled him, punishing him by making him work as a mere spiritual director. The authors of *From the End of the Earth to Rome,* the staff of the *Wall Street Journal,* breathlessly declared this period "a setback in his climb up the ecclesiastical ladder."[115]

Instead of looking through the lens of politics, we will gain a clearer view of this episode by looking through the lens of one of Pope Francis's Jesuit forebears. Jean Pierre de Caussade devoted much of his Jesuit life to work much like that of Fr. Bergoglio's so-called "setback" years; Caussade was spiritual director and confessor for a convent. He died without ever making a "climb up the ecclesiastical ladder." Caussade's spiritual notes and instructions for the convent sisters, archived and treasured for generations, were published some 110 years after his death (would-be authors take heart). I suspect that only history buffs could name a French bishop who had climbed the French ecclesiastical ladder during the 1740s, but many thousands each year meditate on Caussade's renowned *Abandonment to Divine Providence,* also known, more tellingly, as *The Sacrament of the Present Moment.*

Pope Francis may be one of those who have been enriched by reading the work of his fellow Jesuit Caussade, though it's also possible that their similar focus on the mysticism of the present moment came by integrating the same Jesuit principle during their training: do what you're doing. Here's how Caussade put it: "There is not a moment in which God does not present Himself, under the cover of some pain to be endured, some consolation to be enjoyed, or of some duty to be performed."[116] Or, in another place:

> What is the secret of finding the Treasure? There isn't one. The Treasure is everywhere. It is offered to us at every moment and wherever we find ourselves. All creatures, friends or enemies, pour it out abundantly. We could not choose to become good in a better, more miraculous, and yet easier way than by the simple use of the means offered us by God; the whole-hearted acceptance of everything that comes to us at every moment of our lives.[117]

Effective leaders, whether religious believers or not, commit to the mysticism of the present moment. Yesterday's opportunity has passed; tomorrow's might not come; today's is waiting for me.

Reverence Tradition: Stand for Something

If only it were as simple as living in the present.

Let's illustrate with the ridiculous before pondering the sublime. When I was a fairly successful young investment banker, opportunities to seize the present moment often arose after a few Friday night drinks in some Wall Street or Roppongi, Tokyo, watering hole. Those were chances to live in the present, for sure, but also to demonstrate what I stood for, how I thought human beings ought to treat one another.

That same dynamic has been an undercurrent of previous paragraphs. We will all be appalled if the pope turns out to be a careerist hypocrite because we believe integrity is a value worth standing for. And Pope Francis's confession box question to working parents—do you play with your kids?—highlights an even more fundamental value: we ought to love our children and put their needs and interests above our own.

In short, the present moment can never be divorced completely from the past. How I behave right now is an affirmation or rejection of what has been bequeathed by those who came before me: the values, culture, and practices of my spiritual tradition, community, or country.

I read an interview with William Dalrymple, the Scottish-born, award-winning author of several books including *Return of a King: The Battle for Afghanistan, 1839–42*, a subject that won him an invitation to brief White House foreign-policy advisors eager to learn about Afghanistan's past as the United States now enters the second decade of a dubious effort to shape Afghanistan's future.[118] Here's how he summed up the experience: "It was like addressing an incredibly bright university seminar full of super-pushy Harvard kids. They were unbelievably well briefed about everything political and current but had paper-thin cultural or historical grounding in the subject."[119]

Whether or not his characterization is completely fair, it epitomizes the hubris that can afflict our modern age. Like *Moby Dick*'s Captain Ahab, arrogantly proclaiming, "What I've dared, I've willed; and what I've willed, I'll do," we sometimes imagine ourselves the lords of history, nature, and culture. It's not merely that we live in the present; it's as if what came before us never mattered. We free ourselves from the moral shackles of antiquated religious beliefs or the outmoded customs of grandparents; we insist on judging right and wrong by our own personal standards. Enchanted by the new and enthralled by technological progress, we resent anything that might slow it, like curmudgeonly appeals in the name of ethical or religious principles to stop and consider the moral implications of, say, genetically reengineering our bodies, fashioning designer offspring, or inventing whole new "chimera" species.

But where does living only in the present leave us? Not exactly free, sometimes merely adrift and at the mercy of the current; at least that's how Pope Francis expressed it in challenges to his fellow Christians: "A Christian without memory is not a true Christian . . . he or she is a prisoner of circumstance, of the moment, a man or woman who has no history."[120]

When that happens, he said in another sermon, we find ourselves "going from one experience to another without thinking and following the fashions of the time . . . We are seduced by temporariness."[121]

And if everything we decide or create is guided only by the impulse of the present moment, the pope observed elsewhere, " . . . what happens? The same thing that happens to children on the beach when they build sandcastles: everything is swept away, there is no solidity."[122]

The pope who is relentlessly committed to seizing every present opportunity understands that no leader effectively engages the present without some set of orienting values to help distinguish one opportunity as more meaningful, worthwhile, moral, or just than another. The pope returned to counsel that young man only because he was pulled up short by some inner sense of right and wrong, some recollection of the values that he wanted to stand for as a Christian and a person.

As archbishop of Buenos Aires, Bergoglio must have ordained at least a couple hundred deacons over the years. As, one by one, they knelt before him, Archbishop Bergoglio placed the gospel book in each one's hands and recited a simple prayer: "Receive the Gospel of Christ whose herald you have become.

Believe what you read, teach what you believe, and practice what you teach."[123] The hundreds of times he recited that prayer were so many reminders of his own commitment to honor his living tradition, its truths and values, in every circumstance of his life.

Believe, teach, practice. Though spoken to priests, it might as well be a prayer for leaders more generally, whatever their walk of life or belief system. Believe in something—don't be one of the "weather vane leaders" who drift this way and that, easily swayed by the political winds or the last person to bend their ear. The weather vanes seldom inspire us to follow, for the simple reason that they are not leading us anywhere. More compelling are the leaders who believe, teach, and practice—that is, leaders who stand for something. A Jesuit who taught in the seminary where Fr. Bergoglio was rector told me, "I wasn't always in agreement with the way he was doing things, but I looked up to him. He had a vision, and he was committed to it." He stood for something.

"Believe, teach, and practice" is a mantra more easily parroted than lived. Yes, the airwaves may be filled with conservative or liberal voices who are "bravely" trumpeting their beliefs, but often on networks that cater to audiences who believe the very same things; those voices are not standing for something so much as grandstanding, often for a lucrative payoff in book sales and speaking engagements.

But leaders who stand for something out in the real world find that it sometimes costs them more than it pays off. They live through complex dilemmas where the answers are opaque, situations in which conscientious leaders say to themselves, *I would do the right thing if only someone could tell me the right thing to do*. Real-world leaders have to find the courage to act even when they do not know they are correct, to speak when others are content to keep their mouths shut, or to pursue the course of action that leaves them standing alone in the middle when others are tugging them to one side or the other.

More than once during investment-banking life, a handful of colleagues and I huddled to discern our path through a business opportunity fraught with moral dilemmas. Not an "amateur hour" dilemma like "this might be illegal, but no one will know. Should we do it anyway?" Of course not. No need to waste discussion time on the black-and-white calls. Rather, we sometimes agonized over more complicated dilemmas, such as overseas out-sourcings where our perceived obligations to employees, shareholders, communities, and tax authorities all swirled around in conflict, where we weighed the jobs lost here against jobs created there, and where we debated what "decent working conditions" entailed in reality, not in the abstract.

More than once, after we had hashed through the issues and just about reached comfort on one or another proposed transaction, someone would lean back and say, "You know, I'm just not so sure I feel good about this." Two or three others would quickly chime their agreement, with evident relief. Each of us had been assuming from the conversation's drift that we were the only out-lier; colleagues we respected seemed to be comfortable, so we withheld our own misgivings.

Until the first person was courageous enough to open his or her mouth.

I've often pondered those moments in the years since. I was invariably the one with the best equipped ethical toolbox—after all, I had a master's degree in philosophy, while the rest of them might have completed one ethics class in business school. But I was rarely the first to open my mouth in those meetings. With some chagrin, I recognized that being the best educated didn't make me the most morally courageous.

What does make leaders morally courageous?

I wish I knew the answer for sure. But experience has taught me that the morally toughest were often those who had weathered and even been humbled by the toughest life experiences. They had suffered through the anguish that reality is far murkier than the crisp black-and-white text of ethics books. The agony of living through ambiguity helped them find their footing in life, made them better able to differentiate solid ground from slippery slopes. And because their footing was a bit more solid, it gave the rest of us greater confidence to follow them along the path. Leadership scholar Warren Bennis put it this way:

> One of the most reliable indicators and predictors of true leadership is an individual's ability . . . to learn from even the most trying circumstances. Put another way, the skills required to conquer adversity and emerge stronger and more committed than ever are the same ones that make for extraordinary leaders.[124]

I've looked at my life and Pope Francis's through that lens. The year I turned forty, I was living in my third overseas country in four years and had helped Morgan open new offices in a handful of countries, navigate hundreds of job losses in multiple countries on two continents, and transition our company into a wide range of new businesses. That seemed daunting to those of us who went through it, but, let's be frank, we weren't newly minted cavalry officers leading terrified young soldiers to near-certain death on Gettysburg battlefields. Many of us were pampered, well-paid expatriates who lived in nice neighborhoods; we understood the challenges we had signed up for, and every advisory or technical resource that money could buy was at our disposal.

I think, in contrast, of the year Pope Francis turned forty. He was about halfway through his term as provincial superior of Argentina's Jesuits. He had had just one substantial previous professional assignment, an internal job as director of Jesuit novices. I don't know what he had expected the provincial's role would entail—perhaps he anticipated assigning Jesuits to and from schools or parishes, and every once in a while making what seemed a momentous decision, like opening or closing a school. But leaders don't get to choose the real-life circumstances in which they must lead, and, whatever Fr. Bergoglio had imagined and been trained for didn't remotely prepare him for what he faced that year.

Two of his Jesuit subordinates, Franz Jalics and Orlando Yorio, were witnessing to the Catholic Church's stated "preferential option for the poor" by living and ministering in Bajo Flores, a Buenos Aires shantytown.[125] Fr. Bergoglio, worried about their safety as Argentina's political environment grew dangerously unstable, asked that they leave. They demurred. Bergoglio and the two men were unable to unravel a knot of contending priorities and values: service to the poor, faithfulness to one's conscience, religious obedience, loyalty to one's subordinates, to name but a few. So Fr. Bergoglio presented what he, they, and fellow Jesuits would have perceived as a drastic, painful choice: either close their Bajo Flores community or transition from the Jesuit order to the jurisdiction of any bishop who would sponsor their ministry. But before the matter was completely resolved, the situation became infinitely more complex: the two

Jesuits were kidnapped in May 1976 by a military unit dispatched to round up suspected subversives.[126]

As weeks passed without word of the two Jesuits' whereabouts, the stakes became abundantly clear to Fr. Bergoglio as Argentina was shaken by one atrocity after another involving non-Jesuit priests. Parishioners approaching St. Patrick's church in Buenos Aires for morning Mass one day found the bullet-riddled bodies of their three parish priests and two seminarians, clad in pajamas and lying in a pool of blood; a military death squad left behind a note declaring the massacre payback for some twenty police officers who had been slaughtered in a guerrilla bomb attack. In July, Franciscan friar Carlos de Dios Murias[127] was found dead in a field, his eyes gouged out and his hands cut off; a fellow Franciscan lay dead beside him. Soon after that, their bishop, Enrique Angelelli, was murdered when his car was run off the road;[128] he had been an outspoken advocate—too outspoken evidently—for the poor of his La Rioja diocese. Nine priests were murdered in 1976 alone, and overall nearly twenty killed and dozens of lay church workers were kidnapped or killed over the course of what became known as Argentina's Dirty War, a military junta-led crackdown on perceived communists and leftist guerrillas after a rising tide of instability convulsed Argentina during the early 1970s.

A pall of uncertainty and fear descended over Argentina, the machinations of the Dirty War so opaque and murky that, even today, estimates of its toll vary vastly: between 10,000 and 30,000 Argentines were kidnapped, illegally detained, tortured, slain, or otherwise "disappeared" by military or paramilitary forces.[129]

Priests, religious, and lay colleagues working with and for the poor, such as Bishop Angelelli and the two Jesuits, automatically fell under suspicion, regardless of whether they had been known to have revolutionary sympathies—no evidence has ever surfaced that the two Jesuits had been involved with guerrillas or advocated violence; their crime was nothing more than living among the poor at the wrong moment in history.

About five months after the two Jesuits were kidnapped, they were dumped, likely from a helicopter, alive but drugged and beaten, into a swampy field in Buenos Aires. Fr. Bergoglio later made it known that, during their captivity, he had once persuaded a chaplain to excuse himself from saying a Mass with junta leader General Jorge Videla so that Bergoglio himself could take his place and use the occasion to intercede for the two Jesuits' safety and release. No one can say with certainty whether his intervention was instrumental to their safety, whether he did everything he could have during the intervening months, whether he should have handled the termination of their slum ministry in a different fashion or even supported it, or whether he should have spoken out publicly in some way or another.

All those hypothetical questions are easy to entertain retrospectively, from the safe perch of a computer workstation or on a talk show. But leaders have to make their choices in the moment, navigating each day's chaos and uncertainty as best they can; then they go home to agonize at night, wondering if they are making the right choices. But even if sometimes uncertain about the way forward, they remain certain of their accountability as leaders, as evidenced by Fr. Bergoglio's letter to Fr. Jalics's brother:

> I have sought in many ways to bring about your brother's freedom, but thus far we have been unsuccessful. But I have not lost hope that your brother will be released soon. I have decided that the matter is my task . . . The difficulties that your brother and I have had amongst ourselves concerning the religious life have nothing to do with the current situation. [Fr. Jalics] is a brother to me.[130]

This much also is certain: too many Argentines suffered, none so much as those who lost their lives or children, or who were kidnapped, tortured, or calumniated, like Frs. Jalics and Yorio. And those like Fr. Bergoglio, burdened with authority in a torn society and divided Church, were tested in a leadership crucible for which no ethics class or catechism had fully prepared them.

In the increasingly polarized climate that nowadays characterizes political and religious debate, "standing for something" often means nothing more than aligning oneself with a party, ideology, tribe, or faction and reliably echoing its talking points. In a 2007 interview, Cardinal Bergoglio voiced worry that "Our certainties can become a wall, a jail that imprisons the Holy Spirit." In fact, Fr. Bergoglio's stands have confounded those who like to pigeonhole leaders into tidy ideological boxes. Is he the traditionalist Jesuit superior who demanded that Frs. Jalics and Yorio move from the slums into another Jesuit community? Or is he the progressive cardinal who became known as the "*papa villero,*" the slum pope, and who missioned some two dozen Buenos Aires priests to work in the city's slums, the so-called *villas miserias,* its "little towns of misery"?

Is he the Fr. Bergoglio who imposed on Jesuit seminarians the strict daily timetable and house disciplines that seemed relics of a bygone era? Or is he the Pope Francis who himself has dispensed with traditional flourishes such as red shoes, the papal throne, or the fur-lined red mozzetta cape?

And the Fr. Bergoglio who demonstrated unambiguous reservations about leftist activism during the Dirty War period is the same man who took personal risk to shelter leftist activists in a Jesuit community and who provided clerical garb and his own priestly identity papers to a leftist who vaguely resembled him, so that the man could slip across the border into Brazil.[131]

Many who cheered Cardinal Bergoglio's charitable initiatives to aid the poor have withheld applause as Pope Francis has excoriated the systemic effects of greed or voiced skepticism about a volatile financial system that can generate so much wealth yet leave so many in poverty. The much-beloved Brazilian archbishop Dom Hélder Câmara, who suffered similarly ambivalent public reactions after his own advocacy on behalf of the poor, once summed it up this way: "When I give food to the poor, they call me a saint. When I ask why the poor have no food, they call me a communist."

From the perspective of those hunkered down in one ideological camp or another, Pope Francis would seem to be standing now with progressives and then traditionalists, standing for one thing and then another. But Michael Gerson, *Washington Post* op-ed columnist and former speechwriter for President George W. Bush, got it right. "[The] media have struggled to find and apply a simple ideological label" for Pope Francis, he wrote. "Sometimes he sounds like a Latin American lefty, calling for 'social justice' and criticizing 'selfish profit.' Sometimes he is defiantly un-modern on matters sexual." But what's really going on, Gerson understood, is that the pope is trying to orient us toward a sense of vision that "transcends our ideological debates and challenges all sides of them."[132]

Yes, that's it exactly: "transcending our ideological debates." Standing for something, to be sure, but not standing merely for platitudes or simplistic talking points. Instead, he is trying to unite his Church by challenging all of us, as good leaders do, to ascend to a higher viewpoint, to plumb our memory, history, and values with a fresh perspective, in order to perceive what actions our traditions might lead us to in the present moment, whether in Buenos Aires slums, our own communities, our boardrooms, or the Catholic Church. In this respect, Pope Francis is simply following the wellspring of his own tradition, the Jesus, who, it is sometimes said, came to comfort the afflicted and afflict the comfortable.

And Now, the Future

The present cannot be divorced from the past, and the past always bears the seeds of the future. In an interview a few years before his papal election, Cardinal Bergoglio observed that genuine fidelity to a living tradition paradoxically leads to change: "precisely if one is faithful one changes. One does not remain faithful, like the traditionalists or the fundamentalists, to the letter. Fidelity is always a change, a blossoming, a growth." In his own Catholic tradition, he later noted, "The Lord brings about a change in those who are faithful to Him. That is Catholic doctrine."[133]

As if living in the present and reverencing one's tradition were not sufficiently complex, then, leaders must above all commit to creating the future of their organizations and communities. Here's how Pope Francis once described the delicate interplay of past, present, and future that the leader must balance: "Memory of our roots, courage in the face of the unknown, capturing the reality of the moment."[134] Pope Francis will fail ignominiously if all he manages to do is embrace the present and preserve his tradition as an unchanging, static museum piece.

Rather, change is imperative. Change is imperative for the Catholic Church because, simply put, the current trend is unsustainable. Consider, for example, the Pew Forum's reckoning of the precipitous drop in Church allegiance in the United States, the country with the third-largest Catholic population on earth:

The percentage of U.S. Catholics who consider themselves "strong" members of the Roman Catholic Church has never been lower than it was in 2012. . . . [27 percent] of American Catholics called themselves "strong" Catholics last year, down more than 15 points since the mid-1980s.[135]

And consider Cardinal Cláudio Hummes's 2005 assessment of plummeting allegiance in his home country, the world's most populous Catholic nation, Brazil: "In 1991, Catholic Brazilians were 83% of the population; today . . . scarcely 67%. We ask ourselves with anguish: how much longer will Brazil still be a Catholic country?"[136] Such declines—and worse—have wracked one after another developed country, and clergy shortages plague Catholicism almost everywhere, and sex-abuse scandals have damaged the Church's moral authority in multiple countries.

None of these worrisome trends will be reversed by doing "more of the same." Recall Einstein's witty observation: "Insanity is doing the same thing over and over again but expecting different results."

Change is imperative because of the state in which the Catholic Church finds itself today. And, what's more, change is imperative because the Church must function in a world that is rapidly being transformed all around her. Put crudely, Pope Francis must retool the vehicle of the Catholic Church while it is rolling into completely new, uncharted terrain as technology continues its rapid forward march and one advance quickly follows another, in media and communications, robotics, genomics, and a host of other fields.[137]

Granted, no priest-confessor will be replaced by a robot. But a Church that has already struggled to remain relevant in increasingly individualistic, consumerist, and technologically driven developed economies will face hosts of new challenges, ranging from the availability of work, to the nature of the workplace, to the nature of the human animal. What should the Church begin to do to respond to this brave new world? How should it organize itself? What should change as the Church finds its way into the future, and what must remain sacrosanct?

Pope Francis, his colleagues, and the rest of us will be challenged to do one of the most difficult things that leaders are ever called to do: discern the right path forward through uncertainty and massive change by living in the present, reverencing tradition, and creating the future.

Fortunately for the Church, the pope's Jesuit formation has equipped him with both the mindset and "spiritual technologies" not only to cope with change but to lead change; we now turn to these.

8

Create the Future: The Challenge of Leading through Change

What happens if we step outside ourselves? The same as can happen to anyone who comes out of the house and onto the street: an accident. But I tell you, I far prefer a Church that has had a few accidents to a Church that has fallen sick from being closed.
—Pope Francis, Address from St. Peter's Square, May 18, 2013

After his first year as a Jesuit, Tomás Bradley and his novice classmates were assigned to work in the Colegio Máximo, the large seminary then headed by Fr. Jorge Bergoglio. The theology and philosophy students who enlivened the place all year had dispersed for the summer, and the ramshackle old building all but emptied out. But someone had to keep the complex running, and the novices, at the bottom of the Jesuit totem pole, were the logical candidates to tend the seminary farm, man the kitchen, and help with other tasks. Bradley's role? Doorkeeper. Fr. Bergoglio assigned him to look after the seminary's main entrance.

So Bradley manned a lonely porter's desk at what must have seemed like an old haunted house—one without air conditioning at the height of a Buenos Aires summer. Bradley endured sweaty hours of intense boredom, punctuated by the occasional thrill of a knock on the door.

One afternoon two visitors arrived for Fr. Bergoglio, nuns from a religious congregation called the Daughters of Jesus.

Bradley phoned Fr. Bergoglio's office. "Father Bergoglio, two Daughters of Jesus are here to see you."

"Jesus didn't have any daughters," came the deadpan reply.

The young seminarian burst into laughter and hung up the phone; the two nuns looked puzzled. Fr. Bergoglio soon arrived and ushered them toward a conference room; they never found out what exactly had provoked that young seminarian to laughter.

The Church's future may hang on the point of that anecdote. That's admittedly an exaggeration, but perhaps not by much. The point, fortunately, is not the pope's sense of humor (Catholics consider certain of a pope's pronouncements to be infallible; his sense of humor obviously is not). Rather, the point is how Bradley ended up with that porter's assignment. See, he loved the outdoors and had coveted a summer assignment on the seminary's farm. In fact, it would have been a perfect posting: he had studied agronomy before entering the Jesuits.

But he was marooned indoors, in the porter's cabin, not because Fr. Bergoglio was cruel or clueless about Bradley's talents and interests. Instead, as best Bradley recalls after all these years, Fr. Bergoglio said to him, "You don't need to go to the farm; for you, it will be better to remain here in the quiet of the porter's desk, in its stillness." Remember his insistence, chronicled in chapter 6, that Jesuits (and by extension, leaders more generally) need to cultivate the ability to reflect? As Bradley explains, "He understood that we needed to develop an interior life in order to be effective in our mission, in our work" and saw in the seminary's stillness an ideal school of the soul, so to speak, where an action-oriented young man could cultivate an increasingly rare skill: the ability to sit in solitude.

But in fact, as Bradley looks back on that summer, he perceives that Fr. Bergoglio was after something even more profound. He was trying to inculcate, Bradley says, "part of the spirituality of the Jesuits," namely, that "one can't always gravitate toward the work that one likes or what comes most easily; instead, in order to live fully our Jesuit mission, it's utterly essential that we learn to follow the path of detachment, of availability, of Ignatian indifference."

Detachment? Indifference? Huh?

Freedom From and Freedom For

Rendered more plainly, one might call it "freedom *from* and freedom *for*," a vital personal disposition that helps leaders make great choices to guide their families or companies (or even the global Church) into the future. Without it? Well, call to mind your favorite story of a badly botched decision as you read the following paragraphs; chances are, the decision maker was "un-free."

First, freedom *from*. The future of Jesuit Argentina hardly hinged on Bradley's predilection to work outdoors during that novitiate summer. But project forward twenty years, and imagine a hypothetical Bradley (or any leader) so driven by personal interests and desires—so "un-free"—that it undermines his ability to make sound choices. For example, a Jesuit might be so comfortable working in his hometown, so ensconced in a familiar job that he knows well, that he mightily resists a transfer to new work in a new city even though it represents a far higher priority for the Jesuits. Imagine an executive so hung up on his own ego and pride that he refuses to listen to others' well-reasoned arguments against implementing the executive's new pet project. Imagine a hospital administrator so attached to the same old way of running a hospital as a fiefdom that she is unwilling to experiment with a new model whereby the hospital, physician groups, nursing homes, and community-outreach centers would all partner together seamlessly to deliver holistically coordinated care.

In other words, a person can become so unhealthily attached to the familiar, to ego, or to status, or a dozen other internal demons, that it clouds the judgment and leads to bad choices. Fr. Bergoglio was giving young seminarian Bradley a "training wheels" lesson in freedom from attachments, and, as pope, he has been delivering the same lesson to the rest of us, calling these crippling attachments or un-freedoms our personal idols: "We have to empty ourselves of the many small or great idols that we have and in which we take refuge, on which we often seek to base our security."[138]

This disposition of freedom is a core building block of Jesuit culture; indeed, we might understand their vow of chastity, among other things, as a radical sign of that commitment to freedom and availability. Hernán Paredes remembers Fr. Bergoglio exhorting the seminarians, "We've already made the hard decision to leave behind our families [to become Jesuits]. What *for*? We have to *use* that freedom. . . ." [emphasis added]

Yes, we have to use our freedom *for* something. That's the mirror side of "freedom from." Freedom from idols and attachments only results in aimless drift unless it is simultaneously a freedom for some orienting goal. We shake free of our shackles neither to stand around nor to wander in circles but to run for the prize, the pearl of great price, the mission, the sense of purpose that gives meaning to life and work. Note how the previous examples always implicitly embedded a goal or objective: the Jesuit attached to his hometown and familiar work was not free for a high-priority assignment. And the hospital administrator so stuck on the old way of doing things was not free to pursue a better approach to keeping her community healthy, health care's ultimate mission.

Recall last chapter's theme of "reverencing tradition." That concept now snaps into sharper focus. Our orienting mission, goals, values, moral principles, and very sense of who we are as human beings often flow from our tradition, be that a religious creed or other orienting humanistic beliefs. If we are free, those convictions pull us forward and keep us properly oriented, as a magnetic compass might. There's nothing wrong with that Jesuit who loves his longstanding job in his hometown; it's terrific that he's fully engaged in his present opportunity. The question is whether he has become so attached to that good that he can't pursue what might be even more important to the mission. The spirit of "freedom for" would challenge that Jesuit: "Hey, remind yourself that our fundamental goal as Jesuits is to do what is 'for God's greater glory': you need to be freer for our mission!" Or, the spirit of freedom challenges that hospital executive: "Please remember that a healthy community is our ultimate value as health care professionals—shouldn't you be making yourself more open to new models that might best serve our objective?"

But better than these hypothetical examples is a real-life case study of Jesuit-style indifference—the spirit of freedom from/for—and Jesuit Fr. Fernando Albistur happened to give me one through his recollections of Fr. Bergoglio. He started with a vivid image, calling Bergoglio a "piloto de tormentas" (loosely, a pilot in a storm). Three hundred and fifty Jesuits had been working in

Argentina in 1962; only a decade later, however, by the time Bergoglio became provincial, that number had plummeted to only 221. Bergoglio took over as this diminished remnant fought to keep afloat a range of schools and spiritual works. What's more, the new "pilot" looked out at even rougher weather ahead: in the early '60s, more than 100 of Argentina's Jesuits had been trainees in various phases of formation—the "pipeline" was full, and the future seemed assured. By the time Bergoglio took over? The pipeline was empty: from 100, it had fallen to 9. Not ninety, *nine*.

It's not that the Jesuits had been trying to downsize. Rather, the reforms introduced by Vatican Council II in the mid-1960s, compounded by the unsettling, rapid social change of the late 1960s, had convulsed the Catholic Church globally. As the Church attempted to modernize herself amid the wider ferment of social upheaval, thousands of priests and sisters, seeking their calling in this new world, eventually left religious life.

Plenty of religious superiors were paralyzed by the rapid vocation drop and uncertain how to respond or implement the Council's vision. But great leaders don't pronounce themselves helpless in a storm, they navigate through it. They look forward instead of back. They don't grouse, they act. Fr. Bergoglio articulated a renewed vision of religious life and started getting his feet dirty to shore up the Jesuit ranks. Within a half-dozen years, he and his colleagues had rebuilt their pipeline from 9 back up to 44 Jesuits in training.

And, great leaders in a storm, even though they can't see the weather ahead clearly, accept accountability for making tough calls as needed. Fr. Albistur, summoning another vivid image, says that Fr. Bergoglio "didn't have shaky hands" in the face of tough choices, and he made lots of them. For instance, he transferred to the care of trusted lay colleagues a Jesuit-run university in Buenos Aires and a school in Córdoba. Recall the concept of "freedom from" and imagine how difficult it must have been to walk away from prestigious institutions that Jesuits had run for decades, institutions that had been the life work of some of Fr. Bergoglio's close colleagues.

As we've seen, "freedom from" is meaningless unless it's freedom for some greater purpose or goal, and Fr. Albistur proceeded to share that part of the story with me. See, even as Fr. Bergoglio was husbanding diminished Jesuit resources by ending involvement with some works, he was dedicating resources to a handful of new commitments: a parish in one of Argentina's poorest regions, for example, and another in a mining district that was suffering the ill effects of a population explosion. Fr. Bergoglio was reorienting Jesuits to "the frontiers," as Albistur puts it, the places where he perceived the need to be greatest.

He even dispatched young Jesuits outside the country entirely, to shore up personnel-strapped Jesuit ministries in Ecuador. Some colleagues pointed out that Argentina was suffering its own personnel shortages—wouldn't they be better off tending to their own legitimate needs first before sending their precious resources abroad? Bergoglio's response was something that Albistur says he will never forget, because it crystallized what the Jesuits are all about: "We Jesuits are not about guarding people [in our own province]; we're about sending people in mission [to wherever God's glory may be best served], to wherever the need may be greatest." End of story.

Fix your gaze on the mission, the vision, the goal that ultimately draws and inspires; and then make yourself free to race after it, free from anything that might hold you back. Be free. Be free from whatever internal baggage and attachments might hold you back or cloud your judgment. Be free for sound, bold, inspired choices that serve the mission and lead it forward.

Pope Francis has been sprinkling calls to greater freedom regularly throughout his sermons. Actually, "sprinkling" does him no justice: he has been "carpet bombing" Catholics, both as individuals and as a global Church, with calls to greater freedom, to change-openness, and to a future-oriented focus. The man who had to cope with the "tormentas" that followed Vatican II doesn't want to turn back, and as pope he called those who do "hard-headed, this is called wanting to domesticate the Holy Spirit."[139]

This book could easily run another ten pages if the pope's every allusion to freedom were included; consider how the attitude of "freedom from/freedom for" runs through just a few examples:

First of all: be free people! . . . Freedom means being able to think about what we do, being able to assess what is good and what is bad, these are the types of conduct that lead to development. . . . Always being free to choose goodness is demanding but it will make you into people with a backbone who can face life, people with courage[140]

There is a temptation that says it is "better to stay here," where I'm safe. But this is the slavery of Egypt: "I fear moving forward, I'm afraid of where the Lord will bring me." Fear, however, "is not a good counselor."[141]

The work that is done in the Pontifical diplomatic service requires, like any type of priestly ministry, a great inner freedom . . . from ambition or personal aims. . . .[142]

Free for Good Decision Making

None of the above guarantees that Fr. Bergoglio handled every decision correctly during those difficult years as "piloto de tormentas." Almost certainly, some of his many calls were wrong. That's no disrespect to the Holy Father, but a plain, discomfiting fact about leadership: leaders have to make judgments, often amid great uncertainty, under time pressure, and without a crystal ball for the future. No human being can possibly make every such call correctly.

In fact, we humans are often lousy decision makers, as anyone who has lived through the past few years can testify. Think of exorbitantly paid bank executives who doubled down on risky mortgage securities just when they should have pulled back, of people who bought oversized McMansions with mortgages they knew they could never afford, of friends who reel from one terrible relationship into another, or of the raft of politicians who have torpedoed their reputations and careers through sexual indiscretions, and the list of bad choices goes on. "Gee, what was he thinking?" has become the near-constant refrain of anyone who reads the tales of bad judgment that fill each day's newspaper.

Well, the pope makes bad decisions too. In *El Jesuita*, he confessed that after finding himself in leadership positions from a very young age, "I had to learn on the fly, through my mistakes, and, yes, I've made *mountains of them*." [emphasis added][143]

When his interviewer then noted that someone who reaches the rank of cardinal must have it all figured out, Fr. Bergoglio rejected the notion with a depth of self-awareness and frank humility that often eludes prominent leaders:

"Not at all. I don't have all the answers, nor all the questions either . . . I have to confess that, given my temperament, the first answer that occurs to me is wrong . . . As a result, I've learned to mistrust my first reaction."[144]

One billion Catholics ought not panic about their pope's poor instincts. They ought to rejoice. Poor managerial instincts are not a sin; the sin, rather, lies in not recognizing one's poor instincts. Research tells us that overconfidence drives bad decision making. Far better the pope who mistrusts his first instinct than the arrogant CEO who never doubts hers and plunges ahead obliviously.

Even though psychologists have by now pinpointed the most common decision-making pitfalls, most of us pay no attention to books about improving decision-making skills; after all, we are sure they have been written not for us but for those who lack our good judgment. That attitude is called the "overconfidence effect," a prime trap for decision makers. It makes us susceptible to another trap, the "illusion of control": we typically overestimate our ability to control an outcome and badly underestimate the effect of chance and of factors beyond our control. Did you ever wonder why highway and home renovation projects always soar over budget? We can attribute that to what's called the "planning fallacy," the mistaken overconfidence that we can accurately anticipate every expense and contingency that will arise in a project. Cardinal Bergoglio perceived these pitfalls well, judging by his comment that "One of the characteristics of a bad leader is to be excessively authoritarian because of the confidence he places in himself."[145]

The Jesuit founder Ignatius knew nothing of psychology or decision science, but, as it turns out, he intuitively grasped human nature. He had learned the hard way: he made plenty of bad calls early in life. Eager to spare others the same fate, he conceived what we might call "spiritual technologies," wise guidance through the tortuous path to good choices, whether about careers and relationships, business plans, or even the future direction of the Church. Some may scoff at pairing the words "spiritual" and "technologies," but the Greek root of *technology* simply means "know-how," and 2008's worldwide financial collapse made distressingly clear that "hard" technologies like computer-driven trading platforms will wreak havoc unless managed by humans with the "soft" know-how to make prudent judgments.

Pope Francis's approach to leading the Church has turned out to be a master class in decision tools and attitudes bequeathed to him by his Jesuit formation.

"It's a Revolution": Consult Someone

The Church's cardinals invariably present a united phalanx to the world, from their uniform clothing to their well-aligned pronouncements. We seldom catch a whiff of whatever debates may divide them behind closed doors. That's why their outspokenness ahead of the papal conclave was so stunning, as one after another cardinal voiced discontent with the work of fellow cardinals at Vatican headquarters. German Cardinal Walter Kasper, for example, was quoted by *Spiegel* as calling for "more horizontal government of the Church, with more collegiality" and going so far as to say that "The Curia must be revolutionized."[146]

With reform of the Vatican curia topping many cardinals' agendas, what should a new pope do? After all, he didn't come to the job with an insider's grasp of the Vatican machinery. Every veteran leader has at some point similarly inherited an operation in desperate need of restructuring, and every line of approach has its drawbacks. Sometimes we hole up alone in an office and craft a restructuring plan, all the while painfully aware that we don't understand the operation intimately. Or, we turn to a team of insider colleagues who do know how things work—but will their plan favor their group's interests over others? So perhaps we then invite outside consultants, but we suspect that their "customized" solution for us is the same plan they sell to everybody.

Pope Francis chose none of the above. Rather, he impaneled a commission of eight cardinals to advise him on Vatican reform. All are familiar with its workings, but only one is an insider. The nearly unprecedented collaboration was declared "a revolution" by Vatican watcher Paolo Rodari, who writes for *La Repubblica*.[147]

A revolution? Well, for Vatican affairs maybe, but certainly not for a pope steeped in Ignatius of Loyola's management vision. On the one hand, Ignatius's Jesuit rule book reserved extraordinary decision-making authority for the Jesuit general and for the respective regional provincials (a role Fr. Bergoglio had played in Argentina); no Jesuit "Senate" checks and balances a provincial's authority. Rather, if an inspired provincial wants to lead aggressively in a new direction, he is empowered to do so.

Yet, at the same time, Ignatius legislated that leaders "should have persons designated to give counsel, with whom they should consult on the matters of importance which arise."[148] Both as provincial and as seminary head, Fr. Bergoglio was required to convene his "consultors" regularly, a handful of Jesuit colleagues representing varying expertise, age groups, and points of view. When the system works well, decision quality invariably rises. Leaders must articulate their rationale, say, for wanting to launch a new ministry or replace a key lieutenant, and consultors can probe for blind spots or derailing "attachments" that might be clouding the manager's judgment.

New perspectives emerge during the discussions, which further boost decision quality: the research teaches us that most executives, confronted with a problem, tend to narrow the range of possible solutions prematurely. Just when they still should be entertaining a broad range of possible solutions, they have already zeroed in on one proposal for a yes/no decision.

Above all, by gathering smart advisors, the leader can mitigate his own weaknesses. In private comments that were later leaked to the press, the pope revealed that such a motive had figured into his decision to convene the commission: "The reform of the Roman Curia is something that almost all cardinals asked for in the Congregations preceding the Conclave. I also asked for it. I cannot promote the reform myself, these matters of administration . . . I am very disorganized, I have never been good at this. But the cardinals of the Commission will move it forward. . . . Pray for me . . . that I make the least possible mistakes."[149]

That last sentence underscores a critical bottom line for strong leadership: "Pray . . . that *I* make the least possible mistakes." He will consult, yes, but he will own the decisions; the buck stops with him. Insecure leaders hold back from consultation: they fear that by asking advice they will appear uninformed or vacillating, or that subordinates may come up with better ideas than the boss. And weak leaders who are unwilling to put themselves on the line may drift too far in the other direction: consultation or consensus-seeking becomes a way of abdicating responsibility for tough decisions. Healthy leaders are secure enough to seek advice, yet strong enough to accept accountability.

But doesn't robust consultation slow down the process? Granted, some decisions must be made urgently, without time to gather all the relevant data, and leaders unwilling to bear the burden of acting under such pressure when necessary are derelict. But in more cases, the passage of time is not dereliction but a duty for decision makers, allowing the search for the inner peace that can confirm a choice, hence another weapon in the Jesuit-style leader's arsenal.

Consult Your Heart, Not Just Your Advisors

Four months after his election, Pope Francis had still not named a permanent Secretary of State, the Vatican's critical number-two post, its prime minister of sorts. And heads of most Vatican dicasteries, its key departments, were serving only provisionally, "until other provisions are made."[150] And that vaunted commission advising on Vatican reform? Six months would pass from the pope's election before they gathered to deliberate reform proposals in earnest.

Why so slow? Well, before becoming pope, Cardinal Bergoglio was once quoted as saying, "'Take your time' isn't the same as 'let it be.'"[151] He was paraphrasing another key insight of his Jesuit tradition, one that wise leaders learn and rash ones ignore at their peril.

In a private meeting with religious leaders from Latin America, the pope had offhandedly revealed his interior state during the papal conclave as ballot after ballot was tallied, and his impending election became increasingly evident: "I did not lose my peace [of mind (*no perdí la paz*)] at any moment, you know? And this is not from myself, I am of the kind that gets worried, that gets upset . . . But I did not lose my peace at any moment."[152]

Anyone who has made lots of major decisions probably recognizes that feeling. Pondering a marriage proposal, new career, corporate merger, or choice of school for a child with special needs, we assess the case rationally, then mull the facts again, and likely do so a third and fourth time. Then we wait, sometimes for a few hours and sometimes for a few days if deadlines allow. We pay attention to our "gut feeling." Sometimes, even though our contemplated path of action would be excruciatingly difficult, peace of mind nonetheless settles over us and we feel courage to pursue the tough road ahead.

A sound choice includes key characteristics. For one thing, the decision must make sense; I can articulate a logical case that coincides with my mission and values. But when "this makes sense" aligns with "I'm at peace about what I have to do," we feel confirmed in our decision and emboldened to move forward. When, in contrast, anxiety continues to gnaw at us, we hang back, our inner disquiet a cue to revisit our thought process.

Jesuits might refer to that dynamic as an intuitive form of "discernment of spirits," a process the pope has called "a treasure of the Jesuits."[153]

The phrase might conjure up spooky images of a coven of Jesuits consulting amid wafting clouds of incense. But the process is more art than ritual. Recall chapter 5's insistence that great leaders get their feet dirty in the real world because, Jesuits believe, God can somehow be "found in all things." That includes finding God in one's inner life, feelings of confirming peace and consolation or, alternately, of disquiet and apparent desolation. As Ignatius would see it, those inner feelings, interpreted properly, are important guidance for discerning a person's or organization's pathway forward through difficult choices.

Note the attention Fr. Bergoglio paid to his inner state during the conclave. He was struck that he "did not lose peace at any moment" even though he knows that he is "of the kind that gets worried, that gets upset." He interpreted that peace as a powerfully affirming signal. In Jesuit-speak, he recognized it as "consolation": he felt peaceful, even when, given the stressful situation and his generally anxious nature, it would have been more normal to be fearful or worried. That led him to this conclusion: "This confirms to me that this comes from God."

So when he said in another context, "'Take your time' does not mean 'let it be,'" he was presumably counseling leaders to consult their hearts when confronting major decisions, not only their heads, and not only their advisors.[154]

To be sure, consulting one's heart is not so simple as "I really feel like I want to do this, so it must be right." Truckloads of books have been written about the art of discernment. And, what's more, many readers will not share Pope Francis's spiritual conviction that our inner states of peace or disquiet may represent, more than mere feelings, a mysterious means of spiritual communion with God's spirit.

No matter that one's beliefs may not match Pope Francis's, for it turns out that decision science and the management research, following their own worldly paths of investigation, are being led to a similar place. Leaders are coming up with the soundest choices when they ponder quietly instead of acting impulsively, and when they learn how to read their gut feelings in addition to their Excel spreadsheets.

"Accidents in the Street": A Bias for Action

After consulting others and consulting one's inner voice, the leader must act.

Too many of them shrink from taking risk, for understandable reasons. They fear making a bad decision that will jeopardize the organization or damage their credibility.

Did you ever notice how many culture- and technology-shaping breakthroughs have emanated from the dorm rooms and garages of entrepreneurs with virtually nothing to lose? Bill Gates (Microsoft), Steve Jobs (Apple), Mark Zuckerberg (Facebook), and Larry Page and Sergey Brin (Google) were undercapitalized upstarts, not corporate titans ensconced in the well-resourced research labs of behemoth enterprises. In fact, these entrepreneurs often exploited technology that giants like Xerox, AT&T, or IBM knew about and in some cases had even invented.

The entrepreneurs not only had nothing to lose but nothing to fall back on. They forged ahead creatively because otherwise, irrelevance loomed, if not corporate extinction. In contrast, the subtle pressures on those who sit atop large organizations can incline them toward the opposite: risk aversion and an utter lack of creativity. After all, one or two missed opportunities won't doom a large enterprise, but too much risk taking might. Leaders of organizations with strong reputations, long-standing traditions, well-articulated values, and extensive assets or networks of followers worry about protecting all that they have inherited. As well they should: a foolish manager can fritter away in a decade what wise predecessors built over a century.

The problem with that is, the wise instinct to avoid reckless risk taking too easily drifts into self-destructive aversion to all risk taking. And in a world that evolves as quickly as ours, organizations can't stand still: they either adapt to changing environments or slip behind.

So the sense of security that pervades very large organizations is a dubious luxury. The nothing-to-lose upstarts perceive every day as a struggle for survival; they must therefore be creative and entrepreneurial. In contrast, their well-established, lots-to-lose counterparts can live in denial for a long time, barely noticing as they slowly fall behind here or there. That slow erosion leaves the organization in a deep hole by the time bracing reality finally sets in.

Take my beloved Catholic Church, exhibit A of a massive, well-established institution whose leaders are keenly aware that they have inherited a priceless 2,000-year-old tradition. No pope or bishop wants to be remembered as the one who squandered or mutilated it, so the Church's shepherds safeguard its treasures carefully. Change-minded Catholics who clamor impatiently for one or another initiative may be deemed shortsighted and reminded that, while fads come and go, "the Church thinks in centuries."

But that attitude, often meted out like a patronizing head pat for some naïve child, is no longer tenable, because the Church has been losing its treasure. Not its physical treasures, perhaps, nor its doctrinal truths guarded over centuries, nor above all its life-giving connection to Jesus its founder. Rather, the treasure in jeopardy is that identified by third-century Lawrence of Rome, then in charge of the Church's material goods and almsgiving. Lawrence was once confronted by a government prefect who was looking to levy taxes and demanded to see the Church's wealth. Three days later, the story goes, Lawrence appeared before the prefect accompanied by poor, sick, blind, or suffering Christians. "Behold," he told the official, "here is the Church's treasure."

And so it is. What earthly treasure does Jesus' Church possess if not the poor and suffering? And who of us is not in some way one of them? We are the materially poor and physically diminished, or those impoverished of hope, starving for spiritual nourishment, suffering from our addictions or internal demons, or blind to what gives life deeper meaning in a world enchanted with consumerism.

This treasure—the Church's people—has been slipping away. The number of Brazilians who declare themselves Catholic has been diminishing by about 1 percent per year since 1991; the number of Americans calling themselves "strong" Catholics has been slipping by about a half-percentage point a year since the mid-1980s. No company, organization, or institution faced with such steep declines in two countries that constitute nearly 20 percent of its global affiliation can any longer afford to think in centuries.

And the situation is even worse in many of Catholicism's one-time bastions: only 7 percent of French Catholics regularly attend Mass,[155] only 18 percent of Dublin's Catholics do,[156] and this dreary roll call could go on at some length. To be sure, exceptions stand out, nowhere more encouragingly than across Africa, where the Catholic population has soared from 23 million to 185 million in the last half century alone.[157]

Still, the new pope, hailing from a South American continent where allegiance to Catholicism has been slowly eroding in recent decades, is not so naïve as to imagine that Africa will be immune forever to the trends that afflicted his and countless other countries: as economies modernize and develop, Church allegiance and practice often diminish.

Plainly put, the Church's predicament is urgent. The inexorable drift toward ever-diminishing allegiance could spiral into an accelerated slide, unless the Church can be galvanized into energetic, committed action.

Catholics can thank God, then, for another trait that Francis has inherited from Jesuit founder Ignatius: a bias for action.

Ignatius of Loyola exhorted Jesuits to "live with one foot raised," always proactively poised for mission. Hernán Paredes recalls Fr. Bergoglio making the same point to him and his seminary classmates: "We're not Jesuits to hang around here polishing our nails . . . there is work for us to do."

Ignatius's historical context may be incomparably different from that of Pope Francis, but one parallel is intriguing. Ignatius had watched the Church's membership melt away in country after country as Martin Luther ignited a Protestant reform that had electrified large swaths of Europe. In Rome and beyond, the Catholic Church hierarchy first dithered in denial, then overreacted with condemnations and excommunications that only stoked the reform fires. While the reformers disseminated their message widely by embracing the possibilities of "new media"—Gutenberg's printing press—the Church countered not by sharing its own positive message in print but by fastidiously updating an index of banned books. It's an exaggeration, but not by much, to say that for decades the institutional Church was alternately too uninspired, corrupt, unimaginative, or enervated to act.

Enter Ignatius and his handful of colleagues, a nothing-to-lose, under-capitalized, entrepreneurial start-up committed to helping address the Church's unfurling disaster. They had no playbook, but they did have vision: relentless pursuit of mission and utter contempt for the corruption, self-interested careerism, and obsession with personal privilege then rife among the Church hierarchy, the "princes of the Church" in the worst sense of that phrase. The hierarchy's deplorable example had severely eroded the Church's credibility with ordinary Christians by the time Luther and others began launching their very justified attacks on Church corruption.

Beyond vision, the fledgling Jesuits had little more than their commitment to "live with one foot raised." They threw themselves into street preaching, chaplaincy, spiritual guidance, and a range of other works. But when pioneering experiments in running schools succeeded spectacularly, Ignatius pivoted from his scattershot approach and quickly committed the majority of Jesuit personnel to a work that had not even figured in the founder's plans.

Nearly five centuries later, what remains the world's largest privately organized network of secondary and higher education seems a brilliant strategic stroke. But it was no such thing; it was fruit of the fledgling Jesuits' willingness to experiment and to take risk. Insofar as there had been a strategy at all, it was, essentially, "Don't just stand there—try something. If it works, do a lot more of it. If it fails, do something else." Ignatius's proactive posture is well summarized in the maxim attributed to playwright Samuel Beckett: "Try again. Fail again. Fail better."

Pope Francis has also lived through decades of crumbling Church allegiance as one-time Catholics become less engaged with their Church or find other churches that better address their spiritual needs, or turn away from organized religion altogether. And, as in Ignatius's time, decades have slipped by and the modern Church has yet to find effective, replicable models to combat the drift. Granted, the answers are difficult to find: the modern world presents complicated cultural challenges to all organized religions, from individualism to moral relativism to consumerism.

What is more profoundly disturbing, however, is the overall torpor, the seeming unwillingness to "live with one foot raised," the lack of energetically unified initiative or a spirit of experimentation. Bluntly put: this is important, so where is the urgency?

There has been plenty of *talk* about urgency. The brutal facts arrayed above have been well known to Pope Francis's predecessors. As early as 1973, Pope Paul VI was brave enough to name the elephant in the room. He wondered whether the Church was equipped to communicate its Gospel well to the modern world and proclaimed the "urgency of giving a loyal, humble, and courageous answer to this question."[158] But his urgent question remained unanswered, two full decades later, when Pope John Paul II "sensed an urgent duty" to point out the "urgency" of revitalizing the Church's outreach (yes, he referred to urgency twice in one paragraph).

Popes choose their words carefully; these repeated pleas for urgency are genuine, not the hysterical bleating of some attention-starved television pundit. Yet little has happened across four full decades while many tens of millions have drifted away. Indeed, only in 2012 was a modest Vatican office even opened to help coordinate this effort. "Urgency" connotes a call to action, a burning platform for change, yet no honest observer, no matter how loyal to the Church (particularly if loyal to the Church) could rate the Church's initiatives, modest against the challenge's scale, as a meaningful response to an urgent call to action.

Pope Francis, a new leader, now bears the burden of transforming decades of relative lethargy into a response that might genuinely be called urgent; he is challenged to do what his immediate predecessors could not: translate words into action that yields results. Pope John Paul II called for "new ardor, methods, and expressions"; the evidence of that happening is scant and sporadic. Pope Francis's challenge? To turn that unfulfilled call into robust, unified, inspired action.[159]

A Simple, Guiding Idea

That's why journalists and Catholic commentators may have been wasting ink and gigabytes wondering, "What will Francis actually do? How will he restructure the Church? When will he reorganize the bureaucracy?"

The excessive preoccupation with these infrastructure questions, what the pope calls "a church that becomes self-referential," is blinding these commentators to the very real revolution that is unfolding before their eyes. What will Francis do, they ask? Ignite massive culture change in the Catholic Church. Turn its focus outward. Deepen its identification with the world's poor and suffering. Spur more proactive, enthusiastic outreach. That effort to change culture will likely be the hallmark initiative of his papacy, and it began on that tradition-busting evening when he stepped out on the balcony after his election. Make no mistake; he has chosen to shoulder a Herculean task. Few leadership challenges are harder than changing the culture of a large, tradition-bound organization. Resistance to change runs deep not necessarily because of entrenched opposition or ill will, but simply because organizations are complex systems in which individuals get so used to their accustomed roles that change can be like asking right-handed people to throw left-handed.

It's as if resistance becomes hardwired into the institution; change efforts are short-circuited. Consider how faintly those papal calls to urgency over the years have echoed throughout the Church, much less in the pews: I've never heard a call to urgency preached from a pulpit. Francis has set to changing that, alternately encouraging and cajoling his billion-strong flock as he laments that the "life of slumbering Christians is a sad life" and pleads with "couch potato Catholics" and "lukewarm Christians . . . who don't feel like going forward." Well, those strong words haven't resounded very loudly yet either, and those of us who heard them have likely presumed they were intended for someone else. That is what resistance to culture change looks like in large organizations.[160]

The first step to a changed culture is depicting the new one, and Francis has started painting a picture. He portrays a humbler, simpler Church. He wants a Church more closely identified with those at society's peripheries—the poor, vulnerable, and marginalized: "How I would like a Church that is poor and for the poor," he told journalists. He envisions a Church that proactively, joyfully engages the world (and its own lapsed members) with its message.[161]

He comes back to these same few ideas again and again, critically important for any leader. Perhaps his predecessors' calls to urgency were faint, among many other reasons, because they were swallowed up and lost in the wide river of papal pronouncements, sermons, and encyclicals. Eloquent and learned though those words may be, and essential though they are for deepening the tradition, how many Catholics read even half of them? One percent of Catholics? Fewer? Instead, what has eluded us, and what we ordinary Catholics need, is not every answer to every question but a compelling answer to one question: what are we Catholics called to be and do amid the turbulence of this new century?

The answer, though surely not a sound bite or snappy slogan, must nonetheless be a simple, direct, guiding vision that Catholics can grasp and hang onto; it must feel relevant to our lives.

Oh, and one more thing: that guiding idea must be a call to action, which gets to the second step in massive culture change: translating vision into action. Pope Francis's approach bears more than a passing resemblance to Ignatius's activist response to the Church's crisis of his time, and, fortuitously, the pope's instincts happen to align well with best-practice principles for galvanizing organizations around change.

- *Unify the team around a common mission.* When things are going poorly, organizations often dissolve into factions and finger-pointing, so the leader needs to reunify the team around some common sense of mission (as just noted above). It may be mere coincidence that sainthood was announced for the late popes John XXIII and John Paul II on the very same day; it was a fortunate coincidence at worst and clever strategy at best. Both are iconic heroes to multitudes of Catholics, but, to some extent, to different multitudes that overlap only partially. By elevating both these predecessors together, the pope has symbolically invited their devotees onto a unified team. So too, for that matter, do the emerging core elements of his vision: no matter their ideological leanings, all

Catholics can rally around his appeal for a Church that is humbler, more intensely devoted to the neediest, and far more energized in its outreach.

- *Put the mission ahead of self-interest.* When the road ahead is difficult, key lieutenants need to lead the march, not scurry here and there to advance their own agendas. Mission must come ahead of self-interest. The pope knows it; he has railed more than once against what he calls the leprosy of clerical careerism. "Above all," he told recruits to the Vatican diplomatic corps, "be free from ambition or personal aims, which can cause so much harm to the Church, taking care to always put in the first place not your own self-fulfillment . . . but the greater good of the cause of the Gospel and the fulfillment of the mission that has been entrusted to you. This freedom from ambition or personal aims, for me, is important, it's important! Careerism is leprosy! Leprosy!"[162]

- *Don't run from the future; run toward it.* Change is hard for any organization; leaders have to encourage wary followers to embrace change, and Francis has to encourage change-openness among Catholics raised to reverence their millennia-old tradition. He's doing this by reminding us that openness to change and a new future is part of the millennia-old tradition. As he put it, "The Holy Spirit upsets us because it moves us, it makes us walk, it pushes the church forward . . . it's what gives us the strength to go forward, but many find this upsetting and prefer the comfort of the familiar."[163]

- *Be biased toward action and tolerate failed experiments.* The Church must revitalize herself in a complex, evolving world. If there was a sure-proof path to doing so, someone would have figured it out by now. There isn't; the terrain is too unfamiliar. So the Church must experiment, and some of those experiments will certainly fail. The only way to avoid failure? Do nothing. And doing nothing will only exacerbate all those unhappy trends noted above. Bad leaders don't tolerate failed experiments. Great leaders bless them, knowing that some vexing problems can be solved only by trial and error, or, in the pope's imagery, by "accidents in the street": "A church that doesn't get out, sooner or later, gets sick from being locked up. . . . It's also true that getting out in the street runs the risk of an accident, but frankly I prefer a church that has accidents a thousand times to a church that gets sick."[164]

In a Word? Transcendence

Transcendence: that by-now familiar refrain links all these ideas. Pope Francis is driving his Church not to reject its tradition but to focus on its future; to transcend self-interest for the sake of the mission; to transcend fear of failure to embrace the possibility of success; and to transcend self-referential preoccupation with bureaucratic debates in order to focus outwardly.

It was instructive—and worrisome—that so much pre-conclave discussion and reporting focused on internal problems, like reform of the Vatican curia and the Vatican bank. Worrisome because a common symptom of troubled institutions is to turn inward and become consumed by internal politics, organization charts, and bureaucratic reorganizations. Productive energy gets trapped within the institutional walls instead of radiated outward. Leaders in the field start focusing on what's happening at headquarters instead of on those they should be serving.

Yes, remedying the Church's internal problems is important, but doing so will not heal the Church's graver ills. Those one percent of Brazilian Catholics who drift away each year? Virtually none of them are drifting away because of malfeasance at the Vatican bank or an inefficient Vatican curia, and none of them will come back simply because those internal problems get fixed.

Pope Francis was unlucky to have been saddled with lingering organizational dysfunctions and malfunctions. These festering sores must be addressed to establish a more credible, better respected, and professional administrative structure. But Pope Francis can't allow internal management issues to become a sinkhole that sucks in the preponderance of his time and energy. Credit him with perceiving this: he seems intent on maintaining his relentless outward focus on mission. A leader can find and direct a talented lieutenant to fix the internal plumbing, but a leader cannot delegate the task of leading the outward-facing mission.

What Is Pope Francis's Biggest Challenge?

If you can't lead yourself, don't bother trying to lead the rest of us: that theme dominated chapter 3 and surfaced regularly thereafter. Leaders have to start with themselves, and Pope Francis has done so. We've been watching a virtuoso performance of what might be called the "Gandhi model," that is, in the words often attributed to the Mahatma: "Be the change you want to see in the world."

Pope Francis has been modeling the vision: choosing simpler living quarters than the papal apartments, regularly foregoing a thronelike chair, eschewing the papal limousine, and in a dozen other ways. Consider also, as one example of many, his unexpected absence from a stately Vatican concert coupled with his equally unanticipated visit to impoverished refugees on Lampedusa. Those two choices had nothing to do with each other literally but everything to do with each other symbolically: a snapshot of the pope's chair standing empty at the concert, juxtaposed with one of Francis standing amid Lampedusa's dispossessed refugees, vividly depicts "a Church that is poor and for the poor."

His role modeling has resonated powerfully with his billion-strong flock. He enjoys an 85 percent approval rating among Italians, popularity that most of the world's politicians attain only in their dreams. Fifteen percent more Italians express confidence in the Church than did so a few months ago. Pope Francis counts seven million worldwide Twitter followers, more than three times what he inherited. And his words have stirred action: anecdotes suggest that the pope's constant reminders of God's mercy have spawned a mini-boomlet in Catholic confessional box visits around the world; "The Lord never tires of forgiving," Pope Francis said on March 17, "it is we who tire of asking for forgiveness."[165]

His indisputable popularity and charisma are essential to his chances for success. Trying to implement an ambitious institutional agenda is always difficult, even when you are popular. When you are not? Don't bother trying.

All that said, the "Gandhi model" by itself is rarely enough to change large organizations and almost certainly will not be enough to change the Catholic Church. Though personal role modeling is essential for spurring change, it is not sufficient. The new vision and culture change must be institutionalized to be sustainable.

Take the case study, for example, of the beloved Pope John Paul II, revered and cherished around the world, nowhere more so than in his own Poland, where more than 90 percent of the population are baptized Catholics. Yet not even that pope's charisma, holiness, and weighty intellect could deter the Church's sliding fortunes in his native country, where church allegiance started falling rapidly during his own lifetime: more than 50 percent of Poles attended weekly Mass in the early 1990s; now the figure hovers around 40 percent; and weekly Mass attendance in the bellwether city of Warsaw has fallen to about 20 percent, ominous in that this urban center and magnet for young Poles inevitably influences the nation's culture.[166]

The lesson? No one person alone can conquer the Church's intractable challenges.

That's not unique to the Church; it's one of the first lessons of change management. The pope, like any other leader, must enfranchise and motivate a broad leadership group not merely to comply with his vision but to drive his vision, not merely to talk the talk, nor even to walk the talk, but to shed sweat and tears beside him, and, if called for, to shed blood as well.

The Needed Tipping Point of Witness

Pope Francis leads a diverse multinational institution that functions in nearly two hundred countries and is administered through more than 2,000 dioceses, each headed by a bishop who exercises considerable autonomy. Each of them is directly accountable to the pope, which might imply the capacity to wield swift, direct managerial influence. Not so. His span of control is impossibly broad. No human being can manage 2,000 subordinates proactively. He neither conducts annual performance reviews for each diocesan bishop nor establishes each one's key annual objectives. Indeed, some bishops sit down with their "boss" as infrequently as once every five years, and then only as part of a small-group meeting. Many bishops will never have a substantive one-on-one meeting with their boss.

In short, the pope does not pull as many powerful levers as one might imagine of a "Supreme Pontiff," and so, Pope Francis, well into his seventies, is racing against time, because the new culture will take root only if he can cajole, inspire, appoint, or browbeat a vanguard of bishops and church leaders into driving change alongside him.

I suspect this will be his pontificate's great challenge, and while his Jesuit formation stocked his leadership tool shed for many challenges, no Jesuit-inspired implement lies at hand for this task. Recall those long years of Jesuit formation described in earlier chapters. That serves, among many other purposes, as an intense indoctrination into the Jesuit "way of doing things." Jesuits emerge with a strong common culture, outlook, and attitude toward mission; the founding generation even coined a phrase for it: *nuestro modo de proceder*—"our way of proceeding." If creative Jesuit leaders can tap into this shared culture, they can drive change, as Fr. Bergoglio did in his various Jesuit leadership postings.

But Pope Francis's challenge is far different. Of course his bishops and other Church leaders are 100 percent behind him. Of course they broadly agree on priorities, doctrine, and dozens more things. But he has never even met the overwhelming majority of bishops he now manages, and his modeling is implicitly challenging them to approach their roles differently and perhaps reorder their priorities—for one thing, by embracing his own feet-dirty, smell-of-the-sheep leadership style. Recall how Fr. Bergoglio and his seminarian charges sketched a crude map of their Buenos Aires *barrio* and resolved to visit every local family? Well, there are some 400,000 Catholic priests around the world. Imagine each of them replicating that initiative. Imagine each priest, sitting around a table with religious women and lay colleagues, surveying a neighborhood map and parceling out accountability among themselves and other volunteers to walk every block and visit every family, challenging each other just as Fr. Bergoglio challenged those seminarians: "get into the neighborhood and walk it," "get the kids for [religious instruction]," "don't 'comb the sheep,' meet all of them," "visit the poor and take care of their needs," "learn from the people before you teach them anything," and doing all this will be "important for the formation of your heart." That would be a new *modo de proceder*, a new way of doing business, for the overwhelming majority of the world's parishes, a style that would push Church leaders far outside their comfort zones.

What would that strategy look like in action? Well, the pope depicted it when he visited the economically disadvantaged community of Varginha

(Manguinhos) during his July, 2013, visit to Brazil for World Youth Day. He told the community: "From the start, my wish in planning this visit to Brazil was to be able to visit every district throughout the nation. I would have liked to knock on every door, to say 'good morning,' to ask for a glass of cold water, to take a *cafezinho*, to speak as one would to family friends, to listen to each person pouring out his or her heart—parents, children, grandparents . . . But Brazil is so vast! It is impossible to knock on every door!"[167]

It's impossible for the pope to knock on every door in the world, but it might be possible for his billion-strong Church to do so. That's the sort of energetic engagement he is anxious to inspire. Importantly, he imagines himself (and by extension, his bishops and pastors), knocking on every door in order "*to listen to each person pouring out his or her heart.*" Pope Francis is reinforcing the very same conviction that Fr. Bergoglio impressed upon those Jesuit seminarians: "You are going to learn from the people before you teach them anything," Fr. Tomás Bradley remembers him saying, because closeness to poor people is "important for the formation of a priest's heart."

Indeed, the pope's modeling invites his colleagues not only to imagine their work in new ways, but also to change their lifestyles in order to transform the Church more definitively into one that is "poor and for the poor." Pope Francis will have failed in this regard if he remains the quirky exception, that pope who chose to live in simpler quarters and who traveled in standard-issue automobiles rather than in limos. He will have succeeded if he becomes, well, utterly unexceptional—if a few hundred more bishops follow his lead.

To be sure, a great many already do live like him. I've been privileged to meet one or two of them in developing countries, men who shared the lifestyle hardships of their flocks and whose personal living standards were well beneath that of a poor person in my own country. Their witness challenged me.

But then I got home and got over that challenge. I—like, I suspect, at least a couple hundred million other Catholics—am pretty comfortably settled; nudging us into changed lifestyles and priorities isn't easy. We may admire an exemplar like Pope Francis, and he might even provoke some musings about whether we lead lifestyles that are a tad too cushy, given that 1.5 billion neighbors on the planet live in utterly abject poverty. But to provoke change rather than mere musings? Well, that's unlikely to happen based only on sermons about how blessed are the poor in spirit or because of the lone example, no matter how striking, of the pope and a handful like him.

See, Pope Paul VI was only half-right when he said, "modern man listens more willingly to witnesses than to teachers." Yes, for sure, it's witnesses rather than talkers who rivet us. But to change behavior? Lots of witnesses are needed. Most of us will change only when we can no longer escape doing so because we are confronted by such an unrelenting onslaught of witnesses that Pope Francis is no longer the exception; rather, those of us cocooned in our comfortable lifestyles are the exceptions. Pope Francis's challenge is to inspire enough leader-witnesses to create that tipping point.

So, Will He Succeed?

Only a fool would pretend to know. The Church has faced its intractable challenges for decades, and those challenges can't be addressed successfully without openness to change, to creativity, and to experimentation—as Pope John Paul II put it, new "methods and expressions" are essential.[168]

That leaves him with a leadership balancing act. On the one hand, he must create a burning platform, a spirit of urgency that will no longer permit complacency with doing things the way they have always been done before.

Yet at the same time, he must engender hope and confidence that the situation is not dire and that change will bear fruit. Well, could any event be more wildly, improbably hopeful than a dead person who rises to new life? Easter is the very embodiment of Christian hope and confidence, and Francis's sermon at the 2013 Easter Vigil was striking. He imagined the women who approached Jesus' tomb only to find it empty. Something "new and unexpected happens," the pope preached, and this "upsets [the women's] hearts and their plans. . . . It is an event which leaves them perplexed, hesitant, full of questions."[169]

Then the pope pivoted to the present-day experience of his billion-strong community. He spoke about the discomfort of the new, about human resistance to change, and he made a parallel to the initial resistance experienced by those women:

Doesn't the same thing also happen to us when something completely new occurs in our everyday life? We stop short, we don't understand, we don't know what to do. *Newness* often makes us fearful, including the newness which God brings us, the newness which God asks of us. . . . Dear brothers and sisters, we are afraid of God's surprises! He always surprises us! The Lord is like that.

Dear brothers and sisters, let us not be closed to the newness that God wants to bring into our lives! . . . Let us not close our hearts, let us not lose confidence, let us never give up: there are no situations which God cannot change, there is no sin which he cannot forgive if only we open ourselves to him.[170]

Be open to the new. Be open to change. He was speaking to each person individually, inviting each to "start with yourself." But he was also addressing his Church at large, encouraging openness to a path of change, of newness.

Here's how he put it elsewhere: "Human history, our history, the history of every one of us is never 'finished'; it never runs out of possibilities. Rather, it is always opening to the new—to what, until now, we'd never even had in mind. To what seemed impossible."[171] The great leader lives in the present, reverences tradition, and creates the future. But Pope Francis reminds us that the dynamic of humans in time, of human history, is more complex even than that. No one is the exclusive author of his or her destiny, and no one can fully create the future, though many are arrogant enough to try. Rather, if we are modest enough to lead, we are both authors of the future but readers of it as well, attuned to a world that is "never finished, and never runs out of possibilities," as the pope put it.

Good leaders understand that they aren't taking us to some mythic destination where the future stops and change ends. Rather, the leader understands that he and we are on a journey. And so we turn to the final chapter in the leader's spiritual worldview.

9

"You won't be afraid of the journey? Thank you."

Our life is a journey, and when we stop moving, things go wrong.
—Pope Francis, Homily, March 14, 2013

Pope Francis spoke those words less than twenty-four hours after his election, in his homily at the nationally televised Mass of March 14. He focused on three themes: journeying, building, and professing.

Those frame this book's concluding chapter. Life, and leadership, is a journey. We are pilgrims on the way. Don't give up; persevere on the *journey*. And *build* something meaningful along the way, not a Tower of Babel, a monument to your own vanity, but something that betters the world. And build on the solid foundations of your convictions: *profess* your beliefs, not in a preachy way, but by actions that stand for something. In the mantra legendarily attributed to St. Francis: preach always, and if necessary, use words.

Implicit in Pope Francis's journey imagery is an important conviction. Outsiders would consider the papacy the pinnacle of the Catholic clerical profession: a destination, the end point of a lifelong quest. But Pope Francis, who rails against careerism as leprosy, sees it merely as another step on a journey, a shared journey, no less, between leader and led, or, more accurately, between leader and companions. When greeting the world for the very first time as Pope Francis, out on the balcony of St. Peter's, he said, "Now let us begin this journey." That wasn't the "papal we"; "us" really meant us. Pope Francis looks forward to what we might build together.[172]

Lousy leaders don't get that; for them, it's *their* journey, the rest of us are along to support it, and, anyway, the journey is largely over once they have gotten to the top.

The Journey: Do Not Be Afraid of Failure

An earlier chapter noted that Fr. Bergoglio used to dispatch seminarians to teach catechism to children in impoverished barrios because someone who can make a complicated topic "simple enough for a child to understand is a wise person." Well, a wise pope taught about the journey of life during a June 2013 audience with thousands of grammar and high school students. The pope, likely with prodigious input from Vatican staffers, had wordsmithed an elegant five-page address for the occasion.

But the pope did something he has been doing a lot: he went off-script. "I prepared this address for you," he began, "but it is five pages long! Somewhat boring. Let's do something else: I will briefly summarize it . . . And then it will be possible for a few of you to ask a question and we can have a little dialogue. Do we like this idea or not? Yes?"[173]

The thousands of kids approved raucously, but some of the event organizers demurred. They hadn't prepared for this, hadn't vetted and rehearsed the softball questions that a few well-scrubbed, angelic students would lob to the pope. Instead, the kids would be "winging it," the organizers informed Pope Francis, which of course is exactly what the one-time Jesuit high school teacher wanted, to test his teacher chops in spontaneous give-and-take with kids who have not yet honed the verbal edit function that typically renders adult Q-and-A sessions as stultifying as, well, that five-page talk.

One of the first kids got right into it, informing the pope he was, "searching . . . searching, yes, to be faithful. However I have difficulties. Sometimes doubts come to me . . . I wanted to ask you for a few words to help me in my growth."[174]

Before you read the pope's reply, take a moment to imagine how you would have answered a young person's question about belief in God.

And now read on, and, if you're like me, marvel as a compassionate mentor eschews sterile philosophical musings about proofs of God's existence and gentle admonitions to attend church more often. Instead, he speaks about the challenges of the journey, not only the journey that is religious faith, but also the journey that is human life:

> Walking is an art; if we are always in a hurry we tire and cannot reach our destination, the destination of our journey. Yet if we stop and do not move, we also fail to reach our destination. Walking is precisely the art of looking to the horizon, thinking about where I want to go, and also coping with the weariness that comes from walking. Moreover, the way is often hard-going, it is not easy. I want to stay faithful to this journey, but it is not easy; listen: there is darkness, there are days of darkness, days of failure, and some days of falling . . . someone falls, falls. Yet always keep this in your thoughts: do not be afraid of failure, do not be afraid of falling. In the art of walking it is not falling that matters, but not "staying fallen." Get up quickly, immediately, and continue to go on. . . . But also: it is terrible to walk alone, terrible and tedious. Walking in community, with friends, with those who love us: this helps us, it helps us to arrive precisely at the destination where we must arrive. I don't know if I have answered your question. Have you understood? You won't be afraid of the journey? Thank you.[175]

The pope spoke a language that everyone understands. Who, after all, has not known the experience of falling—of job loss, relationship difficulties, struggles with wayward children, doubts about one's faith, or a dozen other things? And who has not suffered the inclination to "stay fallen" when it became a struggle to keep going? Yes, as Pope Francis put it, companions help us get through that. And, as he sees it, those companions include not only the friends, family, and team members who pick us up. During one morning sermon, he exhorted Christians to pray neither to some sterile, distant "Almighty God," nor to some vague "cosmic God," but to God who is *the person who accompanies you on your journey.*" [emphasis added][176]

The pope's appreciation for life's journey may well have taken root during his Jesuit formation, as did so much of his spirituality of leadership. An earlier chapter argued, for example, that good leaders commit to come to grips with their giftedness and failings: the Spiritual Exercises forced Jorge Bergoglio to do so. Leaders commit to stay on track amid life's quotidian chaos: the daily mental pit stops of the examen help Pope Francis do so. Leaders must adapt to a rapidly changing world: the spirit of inner freedom and strong discernment skills render the pope open to change.

And now, finally, his outlook on life as a journey, vital for healthy leadership as well. Why? Simply because the one who presumes that his or her Plan A for life and work will work out flawlessly is bound for despair and bitterness because setbacks and surprises are inevitable. As the architect of chaos theory, James Yorke, once put it, "The most successful people I know are those who are good at Plan B." We set out with imperfect information about the future. Sometimes we head the wrong way; circumstances change, and we must learn as we go. In short, it's a journey, and sometimes we fall. Good leaders persevere after each stumble or wrong turn, and even come to appreciate that they have learned and grown along the way, even through hardship.

The Journey: The Whole World Becomes Our House

The archetypal journey in Jesuit imagination is that of Ignatius their founder, whose Plan A for life—a successful career as a knight and military man—was shattered (along with part of a leg) by a cannonball. A profound conversion experience during convalescence oriented him toward a new path: service to God and humanity. That spiritual journey was paralleled by an arduous physical one; he set off on a hundreds-mile trek from his home in Loyola, across the Basque country's mountains and through Europe's most desert-like terrain. After seminal stops at the Spanish towns of Montserrat and Manresa, he journeyed hundreds of miles further to the Holy Land of Jerusalem.

While Ignatius and Pope Francis would surely scoff at trendy terminology like a "journey of self-discovery," that's exactly what it was. Along the way Ignatius became more self-aware and more committed. By the end of his life, he could look back on one particularly powerful moment at Manresa and observe that even if he added together all else that he had learned during his life, "[I do] not think [I] got as much as at that one time."[177]

Indeed, the journey metaphor so powerfully gripped his imagination that throughout his *Autobiography* he referred to himself not as "I," or "Ignatius," but simply as "the pilgrim." Journey imagery recurs some half-dozen times in the slender volume of *Spiritual Exercises*; trainee Jesuits imagine not only Jesus' birth but the road Mary traveled to his Bethlehem birthplace; they contemplate not only Jesus' Jordan River baptism but the terrain he journeyed to get there. The unmistakable implication: those biblical figures were on a journey, brother Jesuit, and so are you. (So are we all.)

Not enough, however, that trainees like Bergoglio would pray about life's journey from the cozy confines of a chapel: they had to endure real-life journeys. A previous chapter noted that pilgrimage is a unique dimension of Jesuit training. For centuries and across continents, trainees have been dispatched to reflect on themselves, their inner resilience, and their trust in God.

Jorge Mario Bergoglio's novice class also set out on pilgrimage (none of his novitiate classmates remain, I believe, so I could not verify what terrain the pope might have covered and thought it presumptuous to try to ask him directly). But six decades after Jorge Bergoglio's novitiate, trainee Jesuits still criss-cross Argentina on pilgrimage. Emmanuel Sicre recently took nearly a month to complete a five-hundred-mile pilgrimage from his novitiate in Córdoba to the Sanctuary of Our Lady of the Rosary in Buenos Aires. He and a fellow novice set out with empty pockets, one change of clothes, a sleeping bag, a water bottle, and a notebook in which to record reflections from their daily examen.

Sicre's novice director gave him no road map but two clear instructions: walk, don't take the easy way out by hitching rides. And when you beg for food and lodging each day, don't identify yourself as a seminarian. Why not? Well, the theme of humility has surfaced regularly throughout this book, in Jesuit spirituality, and in Pope Francis's vision for the Church. But leaders will act humbly only if they are humble, and humility is a virtue that's more often "caught than taught." So, Sicre's novice director didn't want him fawned over and pampered by pious Christians who, taking pity on a sweet young seminarian on pilgrimage, would offer him their guest bedrooms and stuff his belly with home cooking. Instead, the novice director wanted the young Jesuit to experience what it feels like to be hungry, an outcast, a bit humiliated, and mistaken for a vagrant now and then.

I asked Sicre what struck him during his journey. He told me, "I've never had such an experience of God's providence: I felt I could touch it with my hands. We never went hungry along the way." He continued, "The poorest people received us the best. They opened their doors and shared whatever they had." Recall Fr. Bergoglio telling his seminarians that they had to learn from the poor, that the poor would help form "their pastor's heart"? Sounds like that same lesson is still being learned, decades later.

As they journey, whether Jorge Bergoglio's classmates in the 1950s or these young men in the 2000s, I suspect they occasionally recall that their Jesuit forebears have been trekking South America for centuries, perhaps none more famously than the hundreds of Jesuits from two dozen countries who ranged enormous swaths of present-day Argentina, Paraguay, and Brazil from the sixteenth through eighteenth centuries, building, alongside native-born Jesuit colleagues and indigenous peoples, what Voltaire, no friend of the Church, would call a "triumph of humanity."

True, aspects of the missionaries' work in South America would be considered by twenty-first-century standards to be paternalistic and sometimes downright inhumane (Jesuits, like other colonists, kept black slaves on their ranches). But judged against the mindset of their own era, when European colonizers routinely regarded indigenous South Americans as "beasts of the forest,"[178] the Jesuit effort was almost incomprehensibly enlightened.

They worked side by side with Guaraní tribes to compose music, run successful agricultural export businesses, shelter indigenous families from the predations of colonial slave raiders, engineer crude telescopes and exchange astronomical observations with European scientists, and erect churches and edifices that remained long after many colonial dwellings had collapsed in ruins. All in all, the effort was what one noted historian called "one of the few serious alternatives to the otherwise brutal ethno-centrism of the European expansion over the earth."[179]

Pope Francis surely knows these stories well. As provincial of Argentina's Jesuits, he presumably visited fellow Jesuits working in Misiones province,

Argentina's northeastern sliver. He likely visited the ruins of San Ignacio Miní, where his Jesuit ancestors had worked, and perhaps sojourned farther to the small town of Ruiz de Montoya, named for a remarkable seventeenth-century Peruvian-born Jesuit who compiled the first ever Guaraní dictionary and grammar, and who helped organize an extraordinary odyssey of countless rafts and canoes that bore 10,000 or more Guaraní downstream to safer terrain when colonial slave raiders threatened them.

But Ruiz de Montoya's most impressive journey was a posthumous one. He died in Lima, and some time after, a delegation of some forty Guaraní trekked there, crossing some two thousand miles, traversing desert, scrub forest, and the Andes mountain range, braving unfamiliar and sometimes hostile terrain, all for one purpose only: to ask the Jesuit priests for the privilege of interring Fr. Ruiz de Montoya's remains among their community. The Jesuits agreed, and the Guaraní turned around and bore Ruiz de Montoya's body back home.[180]

Pope Francis has been tirelessly urging his clergy and Catholics to engage the world's cultural frontiers, to seek out all who need help, to challenge the world's powerful on behalf of its neediest, to defend each person's right to dignified work, and to immerse themselves so fully in joys and sufferings of those they serve that they bear "the smell of the sheep." Fr Ruiz de Montoya is an exemplar of the pope's vision in action.

One of Ignatius of Loyola's closest confidants, the Spaniard Jerónimo Nadal, once summed up the Jesuit mindset this way: "[For Jesuits], there are different kinds of houses or dwellings," but a Jesuit's most "peaceful and pleasant 'house,'" he concluded, "is the journey, and by this last the whole world becomes [our] house."[181]

Ruiz de Montoya's journeys, in life and death, lend unique poignancy to those words.

Journeys Spurred by Cruelty

Unfortunately, we cannot pinpoint Fr. Ruiz de Montoya's precise gravesite. It was lost to history in the aftermath of journeys that took place about a century after his death. By the mid-1700s, South America's colonial masters had had enough of the Jesuits and their efforts on behalf of native peoples. Though the ensuing machinations of Enlightenment thinkers, religious orders opposed to the Jesuits, and European royal courts are too long and complicated a tale for our purposes, the denouement is straightforward: in 1767, Spanish King Charles III decided to expel the Jesuits from Spain and his overseas realms, including South America (the pope would globally suppress the Jesuits a few years later).

Crown authorities, fearing pro-Jesuit riots if the expulsion plan leaked, plotted clandestinely. With exquisitely choreographed cruelty, armed soldiers surrounded Jesuit houses across Madrid on the night of March 31, roused sleeping priests from their beds, promulgated the expulsion decree, permitted the Jesuits to gather some clothes and their prayer books, and prepared to force-march them toward expulsion ports. Civil authorities began seizing Jesuit houses, properties, and belongings, destroying what they did not regard as valuable, like the estimated half-million books from Jesuit libraries that were pulped and sold for scrap.

And those Jesuits in Argentina and across South America? They slept peacefully that night of March 31. No such thing as Twitter or telephones existed in the 1760s. The expulsion decree slowly bobbed across the Atlantic from Spain, while Jesuits in Buenos Aires, Córdoba, the Paraguay reductions, and elsewhere continued to teach, offer spiritual counsel, and perform other works of mercy and charity, day after day, blissfully ignorant of what floated their way.

Then the same barbarity played itself out all over again. Córdoba's officials herded Jesuits into the community dining room and nailed it shut as a makeshift prison before arranging an overland caravan to the designated expulsion port. It is estimated that hundreds died during the expulsion journeys. Still, more than a thousand managed to survive the Atlantic crossing, only to stagger around primitive refugee camps in Spain, where, Fr. Juan José Godoy wrote, "If there is ever a little piece of bread, it soon finds an owner."[182]

But Spain had no intention of allowing the ex-Jesuits to remain there permanently. Once onward passage could be arranged to Italy's Papal states, the Jesuits (that is, once-upon-a-time-Jesuits) were dumped there and set loose to fend as best they could—some as teachers, some as priests under other jurisdictions, and many as sick souls who died forgotten. Some years into the exile,

Fr. Thadeo de Godoy wrote to thank one benefactor for a gift, remarking, "It has been eight years and nearly nine months since anybody thought of me . . . in the middle of so much helplessness of hard work and harsh temperament, what we have not endured."[183]

It took decades for the Church to summon the will and courage to resurrect the Jesuits; Pope Pius VII did so in 1814. "With one voice the Catholic world demands the reestablishment of the Company of Jesus. . . . We have decided to do today what we would have wished to do at the beginning of our Pontificate."[184] A nice sentiment, though a bit late for hundreds of one-time Jesuits who had died in the meanwhile, for students in South America whose teachers had suddenly stopped coming to school one day in 1767, and above all for the Guaraní whose settlements became easy prey for slave raiders.

Not What He Had Planned

Pope Francis now lives in the Vatican under very different circumstances from those of his Jesuit brothers from South America who were unceremoniously deposited in Italy two centuries ago. The irony surely is not lost on him, history's first Jesuit pope, that he was elected exactly 199 years after his order's restoration, just in time to help celebrate a momentous bicentennial in Church history.

And all these stories of journey—of Ignatius the founder, of the novices on pilgrimage, of those Jesuits who criss-crossed South America centuries ago—may well have influenced his vision of a Catholic Church that should be ever on the move, leaving no one untouched, unafraid of engaging frontiers, and eager to spread a positive message of mercy and hope. After all, the young Jorge Mario Bergoglio had himself joined the Jesuits with the journey in mind. When a schoolchild asked why he had entered the Jesuits and not some other religious order, he said:

> What I liked about the Society is its missionary outreach and I wanted to be a missionary . . . I wrote to the General, who was Fr. Arrupe, asking him to dispatch me, to send me to Japan or to some other place. However, he thought about it at length and said to me, with great kindness, "But you have had a

lung disease, which is not very good for such demanding work," so I stayed in Buenos Aires.[185]

Like any Jesuit worthy of the name, he embraced the roles he was assigned over the years, and his journey surely included jobs he did not want, including, ironically, the papacy. During that same audience with schoolchildren, when asked whether he had wanted to be pope, he confided to the questioner (and to the worldwide media): "Do you know what it means when a person does not really love himself? A person who wants, who has the wish to be pope does not love himself. God does not bless him. No, I did not want to be pope. Is that okay?"[186]

He was underscoring a hard fact about the good leader's journey: it's not about the leader; it's about the mission. And the mission sometimes takes leaders where they might not have wanted to go. The Jorge Mario Bergoglio who didn't want to be pope has undoubtedly prayed many times over a haunting Scripture passage about the apostle Peter, the first pope: "When you were younger, you used to fasten your own belt and to go wherever you wished. But when you grow old, you will stretch out your hands, and someone else will fasten a belt around you and take you where you do not wish to go" (John 21:18). Self-absorbed leaders never willingly "stretch out their hands" to go where the mission may lead; instead, they follow the advice of a famed self-help guru's recent book, always asking first, "What's in it for me?" Real leaders, parents, teachers, and managers don't ask that question first, and sometimes never at all. They willingly bear the suffering that sometimes accompanies the calling.

That's not to say life's journey is grim or pointless. When Pope Francis told fellow cardinals, "Our life is a journey, and when we stop moving, things go wrong," he was not counseling them to wander aimlessly in circles. Quite the opposite. A person's lifelong journey presents a privileged opportunity to make some meaningful contribution through one's gifts, talents, and attitude. As Pope Francis told those cardinals, the journey includes " . . . another kind of movement in our lives: building."[187] We are all builders, whether we build a more loving family, the skills and confidence of students, the well-being of our neighborhood, or a company that serves customers' real needs. And, ultimately, each has the chance to build a planet that is at least a little more peaceful, just, loving, and friendly because we passed through it.

The Leader's Compass

Some do squander their journey; they build nothing more than monuments to petty self-interest; they tear down rather than build, take rather than give. And so we come to the third idea in the pope's short oration to his cardinals, the same idea that has woven together much of this book: our beliefs and commitments drive our actions. The leader's convictions are the foundation of a meaningful journey, of a lasting contribution. As the pope put it: "When we are not building on the stones, what happens? The same thing that happens to children on the beach when they build sandcastles: everything is swept away, there is no solidity." The pope also said, "We can walk as much as we want, we can build many things," but if our leadership does not rest on a foundation of solid convictions, we waste the chance.[188]

Pope Francis, of course, understands his own journey in Christian terms: "When we journey without the Cross," he told the cardinals, reminding them of the inevitability of suffering in life and of Jesus who suffered in solidarity with the human condition, "when we build without the Cross . . . we are not disciples of the Lord, we are worldly."[189]

Whatever one may think of Pope Francis's (and my) Christian beliefs, any sensible person would agree with this much: only fools set out on a long, important, difficult journey (like life) without a compass or GPS to guide them. The leader's compass? His or her convictions, attitudes, and habits.

Back to the Beginning

And so this book ends where it began: the leader's commitments and the habits that buttress them. "Start with yourself," an early chapter exhorted, and "end with yourself," this closing chapter suggests. Remember Jorge Bergoglio's credo, that short statement of core beliefs he crafted shortly before his priestly ordination? The following paragraphs challenge you to ponder your own core beliefs about leadership. After all, at this point, what matters most is not what I write or even what the pope believes, but what you believe—about yourself, your sense of calling and purpose, and the convictions that will guide you on the journey.

This work ends then, with what might be called a new leader's credo ("manifesto" seems a bit too grandiose a term). Even though what follows is longer than the pope's credo, omitted is what he would consider the ultimate foundation for leadership: one's religious and spiritual beliefs. In fact, such beliefs are not only the ultimate foundation of leadership, but the wellspring of leadership energy, drive, and commitment. After all, no one leads a family passionately without loving spouse and children more than anything else in the world; and no one captains soldiers bravely without believing cause, compatriots, and country to be worth the sacrifice; and no one leads a church energetically unless convinced that it has something uniquely beautiful, true, and life-giving to share. Without such deep beliefs, one might be a superbly competent manager (and we need lots of them), but not a leader. Unless buttressed by deep, life-animating beliefs, then, the commitments below ring a bit hollow.

So, the silence about beliefs in the following paragraphs is not abjuration of my own but respect for each reader's, in the spirit of the pope's tradition-shattering first blessing to the world's press corps, which he introduced thus: "Since many of you are not members of the Catholic Church, and others are not believers, I cordially give this blessing silently, to each of you, respecting the conscience of each. . . ."[190]

Decades of laboring alongside colleagues of every (and no) spiritual tradition have convinced me of this: legions of us, though professing diverse beliefs, nonetheless stand united on the common ground of wanting to bring a wonderful yet troubled world the kind of leadership it desperately needs and deserves. We want to rid our culture of self-absorbed leadership by demanding leaders who serve others before self, and by modeling that style of leadership ourselves. The following paragraphs invite us to make the commitments that will foster this new style of leadership: to know ourselves deeply, serve others, immerse ourselves in the world, withdraw from it daily, live in the present and reverence our traditions, even as we energetically go about creating the future.

For that reason, we will dispense with the warning that prominently adorns those fill-in-the-bubble forms destined for automated document readers: "Do not bend, fold, or mutilate." To heck with that! Please bend, fold, and mutilate the pages that follow (except those of you holding library books or tablet readers). Underscore what resonates; cross out what strikes you as gibberish; pen your own amplifications and commitments into the margins. Better yet, rip out these pages after reading, trash them, and start drafting your own leadership manifesto, so that the following becomes not an end but a prelude.

I will commit to know myself deeply

I believe that I am gifted, talented, and fundamentally good. I do not have to earn or prove my dignity or worthiness; it is my birthright. Yet I am deeply flawed, as often tripped up by my own dysfunctions and missteps as by the many obstacles the world throws in my way. I accept myself, but that does not make me complacent with my flaws or lack of competencies, which I am committed to address.

I am called to a unique role in this world, that is, to lead: to point out a way and influence others, first by the power of my own example, and then by whatever other opportunities and authority come to me whether I am parent, teacher, chief executive, or pope. I can't lead anyone else if I am unable to lead myself, and I won't form myself for leadership simply by mastering job skills. Rather, I must commit to a set of convictions and habits that will equip me to lead myself and others.

I am called to lead. If a nonspiritual person, I understand calling as the fruit of my specific circumstances—that is, no one else enjoys my specific gifts, the specific circumstances of my life at this very moment, or the opportunities that present themselves to me over time. If I am a religious person, I understand calling in a further, transcendent way: every religious tradition articulates a vision for humanity and a mission for its believers; that mission is my primary calling in the world.

I will transcend myself to serve others

I need to get over myself. Yes, I need to be grounded in a strong sense of my identity and aware of my strengths and weaknesses; otherwise I cannot be effective. But then I need to transcend myself to serve some purpose greater than self, in whatever way I understand that concept, whether it's the common good,

God's kingdom, giving more love than I receive along my earthly journey, or, more simply, leaving the world better than I found it.

This dedication to serve is both my one-time commitment (my willingness to stand in front of the mirror and say why I'm here on earth) and my everyday struggle to keep ego in check and eyes focused on greater purpose. The struggle is worth waging because we are saddled with too many self-serving leaders in civic, religious, political, and business life. Their horizon never extends beyond protecting their election prospects, party, power, status, paycheck, or their institution's reputation. By my own example, joined to that of countless others, I will do my part to change the face and character of leadership. Our challenges are great, and we need great-minded leaders to help surmount them.

I will immerse myself in a complex world

I believe I am no better than anyone else, and I am somehow connected to everyone else. I will keep my own feet dirty, making sure my team—my family, classmates, subordinates, or coworkers—knows I am one with them. I will walk the world with my eyes and heart open to the joys, sufferings, and everyday struggles that unfold around me, and, by doing so, strive always for an ever-deeper sense of solidarity. I commit to remain "in touch," even though it is ever-harder to do so in a massively scaled, globalized, complex world where technology increasingly "disintermediates" us from the reality on the ground. I know that my actions and decisions have real impact in the world, and I will accept accountability for my decisions; I won't be one of those who protect themselves when things go wrong by saying, "I didn't know," in cases where I should have known. I will not be one of those who look at reality only through the distorting or antiseptic filters of financial reports, handlers, ideology, television, or a constant social media stream.

I will step back for daily reflection

Though I will fully immerse myself in the world, I know that I cannot afford to be fully "of" the world, drifting on a tide of social media stimulation, texts, and phone calls. Rather, I will set aside sacred space every day to remind myself of my higher purpose, values, and beliefs; to reflect on the day; and, importantly, to be grateful for all that I have. I understand that there is more to me and to life than what can be touched, counted, or measured—as Einstein put it, "not everything that counts can be counted." If I am a religious person, I will pray. Whether religious or not, I will strive to be "*simul in actione contemplativus,*" a contemplative in action who remains ever mindful of what I am doing and why I'm doing it, someone who remains balanced, recollected, and focused.

I will live fully in the present and revere my tradition

I don't know if I will be here tomorrow, but I know I have this moment right now. I will not waste it. The one leadership opportunity I can be certain of having is the opportunity presented by today: with the person sitting in front of me right now, in the problem I've been asked to resolve, with the child I will put to bed tonight, through my attitude in the face of adversity. I will live in the spirit of *age quod agis*, always seizing the opportunity under my control instead of fruitlessly rehashing what is past and cannot be changed.

That doesn't mean the past is irrelevant. I am not a solitary atom, nor the first person to have walked this planet, nor the only arbiter of what is good, true, or just. Rather, I am part of a religious or spiritual tradition, a community, and a nation. Many of my most important beliefs and values were bequeathed to me by my tradition, and I will not only honor them but pass them along as they were passed to me. I have a history, and some of my strengths and values were forged in the crucible of my life experience, often enough through challenge, difficulty, and even great grief. With Kierkegaard I increasingly appreciate the mystery that "Life can only be understood backwards; but it must be lived forwards."

I will help to create the future

Yes, I live in the present and reverence tradition. But in a rapidly changing world, I accept that my call to leadership entails a call to help create the future—my own future and that of my family, of course, but also that of my community and planet. I will look forward to this journey with hope and optimism and do my part to create a future worthy of my beliefs and values. I will strive to be free: not rootless, but free from whatever fears, uncertainties, addictions, obsessions, or derailing baggage might deter me from choices that lead to what is good, beautiful, just, and true.

The concluding paragraph of Fr. Bergoglio's short credo began with these words: "I look forward to the surprise of each day . . ."[191] That's no empty platitude, because, as the pope continues, the surprises of each day include "sin" and even "treachery," not just "love." None of that deters the new leader, because he or she is steeled and energized by faith and hope. As Cardinal Bergoglio once put it, "My hope in God is in the journey, and in the quest, in allowing myself to search."[192] May we feel similarly about our own journeys.

Acknowledgments

I am deeply grateful to all those who helped bring this book to fruition within an incredibly short time frame.

Joe Durepos and Steve Connor of Loyola Press first suggested that I consider writing something about Pope Francis; I thank them for their encouragement and advice as I shaped the idea and throughout the whole process. This is the third of my books to be edited by Vinita Wright, and it would have been absolutely impossible to complete the book in this time frame had I worked with anyone else: I trust her judgment completely, and she is a wonderful work partner—I am deeply grateful to her for her extraordinary efforts. Beth Renaldi and Katherine Faydash both added great value through their detailed scrutiny of the manuscript. As so often happens with books, acknowledgments for marketing and production teams fall short because the manuscript must be finished while their work is still gearing up: all I can do is thank Judine O'Shea and her team, including Andrew Yankech, and I apologize to those others whose names should be mentioned. Thanks to Paul Brian Campbell, SJ, the Publisher of Loyola Press, and Terry Locke, its President, for their commitment to this work, and to Tom McGrath for his support.

Jim Fitzgerald did his usual fine job of negotiating this contract and sharing his advice.

Jack Paquette and Dave McNulty, advancement leaders for Jesuits in the Midwest, responded generously and imaginatively to my invitation to use this book as an opportunity to raise money for a few of the countless worthy Jesuit ministries that serve impoverished communities. I am donating half my royalties to these charities, and I encourage readers to go to www.chrislowney.com and follow the charity link in order to add their own donations to these charities!

Most of the translation from Spanish is my own (and any lack of eloquence is fully attributable to me rather than to those who communicated with me in Spanish). But Sr. Cecilia J. Cavanaugh, SSJ, PhD, of Chestnut Hill College, the noted Lorca scholar, was kind enough to review some of my translations and offer valuable suggestions.

Jesuit Frs. Orlando Torres and Andrés Aguerre read a rough draft of the book under very short deadlines and offered invaluable feedback, as did Louis Kim and Ed Speed. I thank them all for their efforts. This book would have been impossible to write without the generous participation of Jesuits who shared personal recollections and memories of Fr. Jorge Bergoglio; I cannot adequately thank Frs. Fernando Albistur, Tomás Bradley, Alejandro Gauffin, James Kelly, and Hernán Paredes for their generosity and insight. Similarly, two former students of Fr. Bergoglio's, Roberto Poggio and Alejandro Larroudé, also shared insights, as did Jesuit scholastics Emmanuel Sicre and Maximiliano Koch.

Ethan Berman, Ed Speed, Dr. David Hughes, and others shared their experiences of leadership in ways that enriched the book.

I was lucky enough to give a number of talks in Argentina not so many years ago, and through that experience (and others) have had the blessing of coming to know Carlos Gianicolo, Ricardo Moscato, and many others in the Asociación Exalumnos de la Compañía de Jesús, Colegio del Salvador. These kind friends provided valuable cultural insights about their country, but, more important, shared their warm friendship and hospitality.

Many other friends contributed to this book, not necessarily by reading its pages but by supporting its author, and, well, just by being friends. Angelika Mendes offered the kind of support I have never before had in writing a book. I am blessed by the security of knowing that I can always count on the support of my brother Sean and sister Maureen, their respective spouses Netty and Tony, and my nephew Colin. Remarkably, the first time Colin was acknowledged in one of my books, he could barely read his name; now, a few years later, he effortlessly digests sophisticated sentences and complex vocabulary, even while authoring his own riveting literary efforts. And, I believe my late mother and father are with me still.

Oh what happy accident of alphabetical order landed me in 1C freshmen home room with Peter Honchaurk, Lou Jerome, Paul Kiernan, Chris Lynch, and Charles McGovern, friends ever since, along with their spouses and children. Paul and Lou were kind enough to help with title ideas, as did Tom Loarie and Maryanne Myers. So did Barbara Hack, and Pat Hammond's occasional messages of support were worth more than she probably realizes.

This book is about a Jesuit who became pope. I've known, been educated by, influenced by, and supported by more Jesuits than I could name. I thank all of them for everything they have given me and congratulate them on the elevation of one of their own to lead our Church. *Ad maiorem Dei gloriam.*

All these people have made this book far better than it otherwise would be. Many deficiencies remain. For those I alone am completely accountable.

Notes

1. Pope Francis's comment incorporates an illusion to Pope Paul VI's remark that "modern man listens more willingly to witnesses than to teachers."

2. Alessandro Speciale, "Pope Francis' First Day Hints at a Change in Papal Style," *Washington Post*, March 14, 2013, washingtonpost.com.

3. Gaia Pianigiani and Rachel Donadio, "Pope Francis Names Advisory Panel at Vatican," *New York Times*, April 13, 2013, nytimes.com.

4. United Press International, "85 Percent of Italians Approve of Pope Francis," June 20, 2013, upi.com.

5. "National Leadership Index, 2007," Center for Public Leadership, p. 5, centerforpublicleadership.org.

6. *The Constitutions of the Society of Jesus*, trans. George E. Ganss (St. Louis: Institute of Jesuit Sources, 1970), no. 817.

7. Ibid.

8. "Homily of Pope Francis," March 19, 2013, vatican.va.

9. "Meeting with Young People from Argentina: Address of Holy Father Francis," July 25, 2013, vatican.va.

10. Carol Glatz, "Pope: God Is Real, Concrete Person, Not Mysterious, Intangible Mist," *Catholic News Service*, May 16, 2013, catholicnews.com.

11. Joshua J. McElwee, "Pope Francis: 'I would love a church that is poor,'" *National Catholic Reporter,* March 16, 2013, ncronline.org.

12. Junno Arocho Esteves, "Pope Francis to Pontifical Ecclesiastical Academy: 'Careerism Is a Leprosy,'" *Zenit,* June 6, 2013, zenit.org.

13. "Where Is Your Brother?" June 2, 2013, vatican.va.

14. "Pope Francis: Address to CELAM Leadership," *Vatican Today,* July 29, 2013, news.va.

15. "Pope Francis to Brazilian Bishops: Are We Still a Church Capable of Warming Hearts?" *Vatican Today,* July 27, 2013, news.va.

16. John L. Allen Jr., "Dolan: Francis Is, and Isn't, What We Expected," *National Catholic Reporter,* July 24, 2013, ncronline.org.

17. John L. Allen, Jr., "A revolution underway with Pope Francis," *National Catholic Reporter,* August 5, 2013, ncronline.org.

18. John L. Allen Jr., "Pope on Homosexuals: 'Who Am I to Judge?'" *National Catholic Reporter,* July 29, 2013, ncronline.org.

19. *The Constitutions,* no. 67.

20. Catholic News Agency, "Pope Dubs Parish 'Sentinel' for Rome Diocese," May 27, 2013, catholicnewsagency.com.

21. "Francis' Address to *La Civiltà Cattolica, Zenit,*" June 14, 2013, zenit.org.

22. "Address of the Holy Father Francis," May 18, 2013, vatican.va.

23. *Constitutions,* no. 553.

24. Jeff Bezos, "The Electricity Metaphor for the Web's Future," February 2003, ted.com.

25. Alina Tugend, "What It Takes to Make New College Graduates Employable," *New York Times,* June 28, 2013, nytimes.com.

26. Sergio Rubin and Francesca Ambrogetti, *El Jesuita: Conversaciones con el cardenal Jorge Bergoglio, SJ* (Buenos Aires: Javier Vergara Editor, 2010), 118. Translations from *El Jesuita* are mine, with the kind assistance of and refinements suggestd by Sr. Cecilia J. Cavanaugh, SSJ.

27. Jerry Filteau, "Peter Turkson: Pope Francis sets new tone for Curia," *National Catholic Reporter,* April 17, 2013, ncronline.org.

28. Allen, "Revolution Underway."

29. Martin Luther King Jr., *Strength to Love* (1963; Philadelphia: Fortress Press, 1981), 152.

30. Quoted in Speciale, "Pope Francis' First Day."

31. Thom Shanker, "Conduct at Issue as Military Officers Face a New Review," *New York Times*, April 13, 2013, nytimes.com.

32. Kevin Kruse, "Norman Schwarzkopf: 10 Quotes on Leadership and War," *Forbes*, December 27, 2012, forbes.com.

33. "Homily of Pope Francis," April 14, 2013, vatican.va.

34. Edelman, "2013 Edelman Trust Barometer Finds a Crisis in Leadership," press release, http://www.edelman.com/trust-downloads/press-release/.

35. *Helen Keller's Journal: 1936–1937* (New York: Doubleday, Doran & Co., 1938), 60.

36. Rubin, *El Jesuita,* 46.

37. Ibid., 39.

38. Ibid., 40.

39. Ibid., 41.

40. Pope John Paul II, *Go in Peace: A Gift of Enduring Love*, ed. Joseph Durepos (Chicago: Loyola Press, 2007), 171.

41. Rubin, *El Jesuita*, 127.

42. Ibid., 128.

43. Ibid.

44. Ibid.

45. Ibid.

46. Ibid.

47. Ibid., 45, 46.

48. Ibid., 128.

49. *The Spiritual Exercises of Saint Ignatius*, trans. George E. Ganss (St. Louis: Institute of Jesuit Sources, 1992), no. 58.

50. Ibid., no. 60.

51. "What Is It to Be a Jesuit?" General Congregation 32, decree no. 2, 1975, thinkjesuit.org.

52. "Homily of Pope Francis," March 19, 2013, vatican.va.

53. Edward Peters, "Popes, Like Dads, Don't Have a Choice in the Matter," *In the Light of the Law: A Canon Lawyer's Blog* (blog), March 28, 2013, canonlawblog.wordpress.com.

54. "Homily of Pope Francis," March 28, 2013, vatican.va.

55. "Homily of Pope Francis," March 19, 2013, vatican.va.

56. James MacGregor Burns, *Leadership* (New York: HarperCollins, 2010), 461.

57. Genesis 1:27.

58. Ginger Smith, "An Emergency Department Story," *Sacred Stories*, 9th ed. (Denver, CO: Catholic Health Initiatives), 89, catholichealth.net.

59. John L. Allen Jr., "Old Friend Calls Francis 'A Person of Dialogue,'" *National Catholic Reporter*, April 23, 2013, ncronline.org.

60. Ethan Berman, memo to the Compensation Committee of the Board of RiskMetrics Group, November 29, 2005, available at www.nytimes.com.

61. Ibid.

62. Hamilton Nolan, "The Dreaded Viacom Layoffs: 850 People," *Gawker*, December 4, 2008, http://gawker.com/5101825/ the-dreaded-viacom-layoffs-850-people and http://metue.com/ 12-04-2008/pink-slip-watch-layoffs-att-viacom-more/

63. Joe Flint, "Viacom Executives Got Pay Raises in 2008 Although Stock Fell," *Los Angeles Times*, April 18, 2009, latimes.com.

64. *Spiritual Exercises,* no. 140.

65. Ibid., no. 136.

66. Ibid., no. 142.

67. "Pope: No Room for 'Climbers' or 'Commercial Religion' in Kingdom of God," Vatican Radio, April 22, 2013, en.radiovaticana.va.

68. "'Pastoral Ministry Should Always Be Missionary,' Pope Francis' Message to His Brother Argentinian Bishops," *Vatican Today*, March 25, 2013, news.va.

69. "Homily of Pope Francis," April 14, 2013, vatican.va.

70. Adam Smith, *The Wealth of Nations: Books I–III* (New York: Penguin Books, 1999), 119.

71. *Constitutions,* no. 817.

72. A. G. Lafley, "Answering Peter Drucker," *Chief Executive,* April 1, 2005, chiefexecutive.net.

73. Esteves, "Careerism Is a Leprosy."

74. Sr. María Soledad Albisú, CJ, "He Taught Me That Love Shows Itself More in Your Work Than in Your Words," *The Tablet,* March 23, 2013, p. 13, thetablet.co.uk.

75. Evgeny Morozov, "The Perils of Perfection," *New York Times*, March 2, 2013, nytimes.com.

76. Ibid.

77. "Pope at Audience: Counter a Culture of Waste with Solidarity," *Vatican Today*, June 5, 2013, news.va.

78. Quoted in Alison Linn, "What Pope Francis Can Teach CEOs about Leadership," *Today.com*, March 18, 2013, today.com.

79. "Address of Pope Francis," July 28, 2013, vatican.va.

80. "Pope: Homily for Chrism Mass," *Vatican Today*, March 28, 2013, news.va.

81. "Pope: Mission, the Best Cure for the Church," *Vatican Today*, April 18, 2013, news.va; Catholic News Agency, "Pope Dubs Parish 'Sentinel;'" "Pope Joins Rally of Church Movements and Associations," Vatican Radio, May 20, 2013, en.radiovaticana.va.

82. "Homily of the Holy Father Pope Francis," March 14, 2013, vatican.va.

83. "Pope Meets with Heads of Women's Religious Communities," Vatican Radio, May 8, 2013, en.radiovaticana.va.

84. "Address of the Holy Father Francis," May 18, 2013, vatican.va.

85. *Spiritual Exercises*, no. 21.

86. Ibid., no. 235.

87. Ibid.

88. Gerard Manley Hopkins, "God's Grandeur," in *The Norton Anthology of English Literature*, ed. M. H. Abrams (New York: W. W. Norton, 1968), 2:1433.

89. "Address of Pope Francis to the Students of the Jesuit Schools of Italy and Albania," June 7, 2013, vatican.va.

90. "Counter a Culture of Waste," June 5.

91. *Spiritual Exercises*, no. 54.

92. Glatz, "Pope: God Is Real,"; "Pope: Our small daily encounters with Christ," *The Vatican Today*, April 18, 2013, news.va.

93. "Address of the Holy Father Francis," May 18, 2013, vatican.va.

94. Homily March 28.

95. "Pope Francis Calls Newspaper Kiosk to Cancel Order," BBC News, March 22, 2013, bbc.co.uk.

96. Catholic News Agency, "Letter from Pope to Jesuit Brother Highlights Gratitude," April 26, 2013, catholicnewsagency.com.

97. Steven Sauter et al., "Stress . . . at Work" (Department of Health and Human Services Publication No. 99–101, National Institute for Occupational Safety and Health, Centers for Disease Control and Prevention, Atlanta), cdc.gov.

98. *Constitutions*, no. 547.

99. William J. Young, SJ, *Letters of St. Ignatius of Loyola* (Chicago: Loyola Press, 1959), 59, 401; Joseph de Guibert, SJ, *The Jesuits: Their Spiritual Doctrine and Practice, a Historical Study*, ed. George E. Ganss, SJ, trans. William J. Young, SJ (Chicago: Institute of Jesuit Sources, 1964), 102.

100. Joshua J. McElwee, "Vatican Religious Prefect: 'I Was Left Out of LCRW Finding,'" *National Catholic Reporter*, May 5, 2013, ncronline.org.

101. Heike Bruch and Sumantra Ghoshal, "Beware the Busy Manager," *Harvard Business Review*, February 2002, hbr.org.

102. Jonathan Gosling and Henry Mintzberg, "The Five Minds of a Manager," *Harvard Business Review*, November 2003, hbr.org.

103. "Are You Working Too Hard? A Conversation with Herbert Benson, M.D.," in *Harvard Business Review on Bringing Your Whole Self to Work* (Boston: Harvard Business School Publishing, 2008), 78.

104. Rubin, *El Jesuita*, 123.

105. Ibid.

106. "Rally of Church Movements," Vatican Radio.

107. *Constitutions*, no. 582.

108. Jorge Mario Bergoglio and Abraham Skorka, *Sobre el cielo y la tierra* (Buenos Aires: Editorial Sudamericana, 2012).

109. Ibid., 66–67.

110. Pope John Paul II, "Opening Address of the Nineteenth General Assembly of CELAM," 9 March 1983, usccb.org.

111. Rubin, *El Jesuita*, 68.

112. Ibid.

113. Ibid.

114. Ibid., 37.

115. Staff of the *Wall Street Journal, Pope Francis: From the End of the Earth to Rome* (New York: HarperCollins, 2013).

116. Jean Pierre Caussade, SJ, "The Life of God in the Soul," in *Abandonment to Divine Providence* (1921; Mineola, NY: Dover Publications, 2008), 19.

117. Andrew Harvey, ed., *Teaching of the Christian Mystics* (Boston: Shambhala Publications, 1998).

118. William Dalrymple, *Return of a King: The Battle for Afghanistan, 1839–42* (New York: Knopf, 2013).

119. Matt Wade, "Parallels Pulled from the Past Mistakes of War," *Sydney Morning Herald*, May 25–26, 2013, smh.com.au.

120. "Pope at Mass: The Holy Spirit and Historical Memory," *Vatican Today*, May 13, 2013, news.va.

121. Vatican Insider Staff, "Francis: 'We cannot be adolescents forever,'" *Vatican Insider,* May 5, 2013, vaticaninsider.lastampa.it.

122. "Homily of the Holy Father Pope Francis," March 14, 2013, vatican.va.

123. Pontifical North American College, "What Happens during the Ceremony," pnac.org.

124. Warren G. Bennis and Robert J. Thomas, "Crucibles of Leadership," *Harvard Business Review*, September 2002, hbr.org.

125. Pontifical Council for Justice and Peace, *Compendium of the Social Doctrine of the Church*, vatican.va.

126. Details surrounding the kidnappings of the priests and Fr. Bergoglio's role have been the subject of some dispute. A brief general overview of the events and the counter-charges can be found in the following: Uki Goñi, "The New Pope and Argentina's 'Disappeared' of the Dirty War," *Time,* March 14, 2013, time.com.

127. Paolo Mastrolilli, "Argentinean dictatorship victim could be first figure to be beatified by Pope Francis," *Vatican Insider,* March 19, 2013, vaticaninsider.lastampa.it.

128. Jude Webber, "Argentine church remembers bishop killed during dictatorship," *Catholic News Service,* August 7, 2006, catholicnews.com.

129. *Encyclopedia Britannica,* online ed., s.v. "Dirty War".

130. Andrea Tarquini, "Letters Indicate Pope's Innocence concerning Alleged Involvement with Argentine Dictatorial Regime," *Aleteia*, March 20, 2013, aleteia.org.

131. Simon Romero and William Neuman, "Starting a Papacy, Amid Echoes of a Dirty War," *New York Times,* March 17, 2013.

132. Michael Gerson, "Pope Francis Provides Inspiration for All Faiths," *Washington Post*, June 6, 2013, washingtonpost.com.

133. Stefania Falasca, "What I Would Have Said at the Consistory: An Interview with Cardinal Jorge Mario Bergoglio, Archbishop of Buenos Aires," *30 Days*, November 2007, 30giorni.it.

134. Robert Moynihan, *Pray for Me: The Life and Spiritual Vision of Pope Francis, First Pope from the Americas* (New York: Image, 2013), 209. Moynihan attributes the quote to "Remarks, June 28, 2003."

135. Pew Research Religion and Public Life Project, "'Strong' Catholic Identity at a Four-Decade Low in U.S.," March 13, 2013, pewforum.org.

136. Quoted in Documentation Information Catholiques Internationales, "Brazil: The Number of Catholics at Its Lowest," October 1, 2011, dici.org.

137. James Manyika, Michael Chui, Jacques Bughin, Richard Dobbs, Peter Bisson, and Alex Marrs, "Disruptive technologies: Advances that will transform life, business, and the global economy," McKinsey Global Institute, May 2013.

138. "Homily of Pope Francis," April 14, 2013, vatican.va.

139. Cindy Wooden, "Pope Francis says Catholics still need to enact teachings of Vatican II," *Catholic News Service*, April 16, 2013, catholicnews.com.

140. "Address to Students," June 7.

141. "Pope at Mass: Courage in Spite of Our Weaknesses," *Vatican Today*, July 2, 2013, news.va.

142. Catholic News Agency, "Pope to future diplomats: 'don't be ridiculous,'" May 27, 2013, catholicnewsagency.com.

143. Rubin, *El Jesuita*, 52–53.

144. Ibid.

145. Andrea Tornielli, *Francis: Pope of a New World*, trans. William J. Melcher (San Francisco: Ignatius Press, 2013), loc. 1688.

146. Peter Wensierski, "Catholic Laundry: Bishops Decry State of Church on Eve of Conclave," *Spiegel Online*, spiegel.de.

147. Pianigiani, "Francis Names Advisory Panel."

148. *Constitutions*, no. 810.

149. William Oddie, "The Holy Father Says He Is Too 'Disorganised' to Reform the Roman Curia: But the Corruption Has to Be Driven Out—What He Needs Is a Godly Hit Man," *Catholic Herald*, June 20, 2013, catholicherald.co.uk.

150. John L. Allen Jr., "Francis drops first hint that reform may be real," *National Catholic Reporter*, March 16, 2013, ncronline.org.

151. Cathleen Falsani, "Pope Francis Quotes On Celibacy, Women, God And More," *HuffingtonPost.com*, May 24, 2013.

152. "Pope to Latin American Religious: Full text," *Rorate Caeli*, rorate-caeli.blogspot.com.

153. "Address to *La Civiltà Cattolica*."

154. Falsani, "Pope Francis Quotes."

155. "France's 'brutal' loss of faith," *The Tablet*, October 19, 2012, thetablet.co.uk.

156. Barb Fraze, "Dublin archbishop says Catholics not passing on faith to young people," *Catholic News Service,* May 17, 2011, catholicnews.com.

157. Annuarium Statisticum Ecclesiae, Annuario Pontificio, quoted in Matthew E. Bunson, *Pope Francis* (Our Sunday Visitor, 2013), p. 175.

158. Pope Paul VI, *Evangelii nuntiandi*, vatican.va.

159. Pope John Paul II, "Address to CELAM"

160. "General Audience," April 24, 2013, vatican.va.

161. McElwee, "A Church That Is Poor."

162. Esteves, "Careerism Is a Leprosy,"

163. Thomas C. Fox, "Francis: Vatican II 'a beautiful work of the Holy Spirit,'" *National Catholic Reporter,* April 16, 2013, ncronline.org.

164. Michael Sean Winters, "Bishop: CCHD Brings Gospel to Struggling Communities," *National Catholic Reporter*, July 2, 2013, ncronline.org.

165. "Angelus," March 17, 2013, vatican.va.

166. Donald Snyder, "As church attendance drops, Europe's most Catholic country seeks modern pope," *NBC News,* March 5, 2013, nbcnews.com.

167. "Address of Pope Francis," July 25, 2013, vatican.va.

168. Pope John Paul II, "Address to CELAM," March 9.

169. "Homily of Pope Francis," March 30, 2013, vatican.va.

170. Ibid.

171. Cathleen Falsani, "One pope, two books, countless opinions," *Washington Post,* May 23, 2013, washingtonpost.com.

172. "Pope Francis: His First Words," *Vatican Today*, March 13, 2013, news.va.

173. "Address to Students," June 7.

174. Ibid.

175. Ibid.

176. "Pope at Mass: How to Pray the Our Father," Vatican Radio, June 20, 2013, en.radiovaticana.va.

177. *A Pilgrim's Testament: The Memoirs of Ignatius of Loyola, As Faithfully Transcribed by Luís Gonçalves da Câmara*, trans. Parmananda R. Divarkar (St. Louis: Institute of Jesuit Sources, 1995), 30. This work is generally known simply as the Autobiography.

178. C. R. Boxer, *Race Relations in the Portuguese Colonial Empire, 1415–1825* (Oxford, UK: Clarendon Press, 1963), 96.

179. Charles E. Ronan, SJ, and Bonnie B. C. Oh, eds., *East Meets West: The Jesuits in China, 1582–1773* (Chicago: Loyola Press, 1988), xxxiii.

180. *The Spiritual Conquest: Accomplished by the Religious of the Society of Jesus in the Provinces of Paraguay, Paraná, Uruguay, and Tape,* written by Father Antonio Ruiz de Montoya of the same Society (1639); Introduced by C.J. McNaspy, SJ (St. Louis: Institute of Jesuit Sources), p. 21.

181. John J. O'Malley, SJ, "To Travel to Any Part of the World: Jerónimo Nadal and the Jesuit Vocation," *Studies in the Spirituality of Jesuits* 16, no. 2 (March 1984): 8.

182. *Ad Maiorem Dei Gloriam: The Expulsion of the Jesuits from Chile and their Journey into Exile,* Alejandra L. McCall, Senior Thesis, University of North Carolina at Asheville, 2008. And it is located online here: toto.lib.unca.edu. I am indebted to Alejandra L. McCall, whose thesis on the expulsion of the Jesuits from parts of South America included

the quotes from Jesuits on this page and the following; the translations from the Spanish are hers.

183. Father Thadeo de Godoy to Don Joseph Antonio Acosta, July 15, 1776, in *Fuente americana de la historia argentina: Descripción de cuyo, cartas de los Jesuitas mendocinos*, ed. Juan Draghi Lucero (Mendoza, Argentina: Best Hermanos, 1940), 146.

184. Jean Lacouture, *Jesuits: A Multibiography*, trans. Jeremy Leggatt (Washington, DC: Counterpoint, 1995), 328.

185. "Address to Students," June 7.

186. Ibid.

187. "Homily of the Holy Father Pope Francis," March 14, 2013, vatican.va.

188. Ibid.

189. Ibid.

190. "Address of the Holy Father Pope Francis," March 16, 2013, vatican.va.

191. Rubin, *El Jesuita,* 128.

192. Andrea Tornielli, *Francis, Pope of a New World*, trans, William J. Melcher (San Francisco: Ignatius Press, 2013), loc. 1669.

About the Author

Chris Lowney, a former Jesuit seminarian, served as a Managing Director at J. P. Morgan & Co. on three continents. He currently chairs the board of Catholic Health Initiatives, one of the nation's largest health care systems. Author of the bestselling *Heroic Leadership*, he speaks widely on leadership, corporate ethics, and decision making, and has been featured in *Forbes*, *Harvard Business Review*, *Fast Company*, and the *Wall Street Journal*, among others. Lowney is donating half of his royalties from this book to schools and health care programs serving impoverished communities in developing countries. Visit www.chrislowney.com to learn more.

Also by Chris Lowney

Heroic Leadership
Best Practices from a 450-Year-Old Company That Changed the World

Hardcover • 1816-3 • $24.95
Paperback • 2115-6 • $16.95

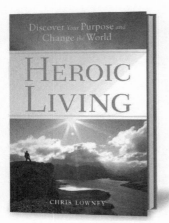

Heroic Living
Discover Your Purpose and Change the World

Hardcover • 2442-3 • $22.95
Paperback • 3295-4 • $14.95

LOYOLAPRESS.
A JESUIT MINISTRY

Continue the Conversation

If you enjoyed this book, then connect with Loyola Press to continue the conversation, engage with other readers, and find out about new and upcoming books from your favorite spiritual writers.

Visit us at **LoyolaPress.com** to create an account and register for our newsletters.

Or scan the code on the left with your smartphone.

Connect with us through:

 Facebook
facebook.com
/loyolapress

 Twitter
twitter.com
/loyolapress

 YouTube
youtube.com
/loyolapress

Ignatian Spirituality Online

Other Ignatian Titles:

- **What Is Ignatian Spirituality?**
  Paperback | 2718-9 | $12.95

- **A Simple, Life-Changing Prayer**
  Paperback | 3535-1 | $9.95

- **Radical Compassion**
  Paperback | 2000-5 | $17.95

TO ORDER: Call 800.621.1008, visit www.loyolapress.com/store
or visit your local bookseller.